# On the Wings of Shekhinah

## Rediscovering Judaism's Divine Feminine

Rabbi Léah Novick

QUEST

BOOKS

Theosophical Publishing House
Wheaton, Illinois • Chennai, India

Quest Books
Theosophical Publishing House
P.O. Box 270
Wheaton, IL 60187-0270

www.questbooks.net

The author gratefully acknowledges permission to reproduce the following works:

Cover image: *Miriam* © Yoram Raanan, www.yoramraanan.com

"B'Ruchot Habaot" (p. 128) Words and music by Debbie Friedman, The Farf Music,
ASCAP. "A Prayer to the Shekhinah" (p. 137) reprinted by permission of Alicia Ostriker,
*The Nakedness of the Fathers: Biblical Visions and Revisions* (New Brunswick, NJ:
Rutgers University Press, 1992). "Modern Blessing for the Sabbath before the New
Moon" (p. 172) by Cantor Linda Hirschorn and "Sanctifying the New Moon" (p. 172) by
Rabbi Geela Rayzel Raphael quoted in Susan Berrin, ed., *Celebrating the New Moon: A
Rosh Chodesh Anthology*. Northvale, NJ: Aronson, 1996. "AYL NA REFA NA LA" (p. 183)
by Alan Scott Bachman.

Cover design, book design, and typesetting by Beth Hansen-Winter

**Library of Congress Cataloging-in-Publication Data**
Novick, Léah.
On the wings of Shekhinah: rediscovering Judaism's divine feminine / Léah Novick.—
1st Quest ed.
   p.   cm.
Includes bibliographical references and index.
ISBN 978-0-8356-0861-9
1. God (Judaism). 2. Feminism—Religious aspects—Judaism. 3. Presence of God.
4. Femininity of God. 5. Spritual life—Judaism. I. Title.
BM610.N68 2008
296.3'112—dc22                          2008013553

5   4   3   2   1   *   08   09   10   11   12

Printed in the United States of America

# Dedication

To my beloved rebbe and patient teacher,
Rabbi Zalman Schachter-Shalomi,
who saw my path to Shekhinah even before I did

# Contents

# Preface

*I* offer this book as an appetizer, or what my grandmother Rochel Feige would have called in Yiddish *ah fohrshpeiz*. It is a tribute to the complex and brilliant world of Jewish sacred commentary. I stand in awe of those who came before me and devoted their lives to this exploration, and I bow with respect to the contemporary scholars who continue to study more deeply than I am able. I know I cannot do full justice to the scholarship that went into the evolution of the many faces and visions of the Shekhinah. However, I hope that this volume helps the reader understand that the inner vision of the Cosmic Mother has been with the Jewish people for thousands of years and continues to find new forms of expression.

Intentionally, I have not dealt with the whole area of scholarship that connects Shekhinah to the Wisdom tradition of the Proverbs and Ben Sira. That rich vein of literature, which has been covered by many gifted authors, is a different path than the one I have followed in tracing Shekhinah's presence through Jewish history.

Much has also been written about the potential connection of that literature to the Gnostic tradition. The great Gershom Scholem and other profound intellectuals have devoted significant discussion and analysis to the possible relationship of the Jewish Divine Feminine to Eastern philosophy. Contemporary scholars like Peter Schafer in Germany and Arthur Green have tried to make a case for the Marianic influence, dating the emergence of the Divine Feminine in the Zohar to the time in medieval Europe when veneration of the Virgin Mary was powerful. Such conversations are available for those who wish to take that road. For me, that line of intellectual analysis has felt like a detour from my own essential knowing of Shekhinah from within.

I have also not dealt with the mysterious experiences of the Merkavah (chariot mystics) of the first and second centuries, whose visions in their amazing spiritual journeys through the heavenly palaces emulated those of Ezekiel. Little in their literature specifically names Shekhinah, though it certainly hints that they brought her energy back with them from the higher realms.

Since the presence of Shekhinah in Jewish history is still not a topic being taught in most conventional Jewish settings, my goal is to make that information, which I have condensed considerably, more accessible for the lay reader. I present this material as an act of Holy Chutzpah. My defense is the commitment to bring Shekhinah back to this earth, in our time, and to celebrate the Divine Presence as I experience her in nature, by living in a state of greater openness and simplicity. The absence of the female voice and perspective in history has been part of a larger imbalance reflected in the chaotic and dangerous state of our planet. I continue to hope for a perspective that supports the full reemergence of the Great Mother and allows for a harmonious and integrated future for all people.

# Acknowledgments

With profound gratitude to:

Shekhinah, who has graced me with Her Presence and sent emissaries—human and divine—to help bring my insights into written form.

Parents, grandparents, and ancestors, whose deep faith and devotion to Judaism created the pathway.

My three amazing children—Mindy, David, and Noah—and five beautiful grandchildren—Hadas, Ayelet, Shoshana, Yonah, and Hanan—who radiate the light into the future.

Rabbi Zalman Schachter-Shalomi, Master Teacher of Jewish Renewal, who welcomed me into his circle of disciples.

Dr. Daniel Matt and Rabbi Miles Krassen, who illuminate the study of Zohar and Chasidism.

Sri Mata Amritanandamayi Devi Ammachi, who embodies Shekhinah's love for all beings.

Devoted colleagues Rabbi Ayla Grafstein, Dr. Bill Little, and Reda Rackley, who provided inspiration and support.

My beloved Soul Memory teacher, Ellen Kaufman Dosick, and loyal soul sister June Sinclair, who have sustained me through many challenges.

Sri Karunamayi, who radiates the Mother's creativity and love.

Soul brother David Cushing Fuess, who keeps me on the path of joy.

Shekhinah "support team": Susan Felix, Ljuba Davis, Helena Foster, and Corey Hansen-Joseph, who provide loving care and hospitality.

Shekhinah's musicians, who have accompanied me on the journey: Alan and Andalin Bachman, Sophia Roberts, Alisa Fineman, Geela Rayzel Raphael, and Shana Winokur.

Sacred artists who wrapped me in glorious color : Shonna Husbands-Hankin, Sandy Pond, and Sofanya.

Ruach Ha Aretz: Rabbis Nadya and Victor Gross, and all who share our dream of creating spiritual community.

Great souls who inspired and sustained Beit Shekhinah but who have passed on: Ruti Hafsadi, Dov Ben Khayyim, Rabbi David Wolfe-Blank, Ursula Sherman, and Helene Goodwin.

Friends and associates in Aleph, Aquarian Minyan, Beit Shekhinah, Chadeysh Yameynu, Congregation Beth Israel, Eyshet Hazon, Kehillah, Ohalah Rabbinical Association, Ruach Ha Aretz, Ruach Hamidbar, Shabbos in Carmel, Spirit of the Earth, and many other spiritual groups along the way who believed in my ability to transmit Shekhinah's essence.

Eliahu Eckelberg, talented treasurer, Ruach Hamidbar, Scottsdale, Arizona.

Noah Novick, who provided technology and resources.

Marvelous Macintosh maven Michael Brenner.

Julia Gilden and Sarita Chavez Silverman, who helped shape the book's outline, and Raffie Cohn, who gave creative input.

Rabbis Wayne Dosick and Sara Leya Schley, who offered critical insights and wise counsel.

Aleph Rabbinical students: Sue Morningstar, assistance with quotations; Jeff Schulman, Talmudic sources; (Shifra) Janet Tobacman, bibliography.

The superb team at Quest Publications:

Publications Manager Sharron Dorr, whose keen judgment and decision making has made the completion of this book a reality.

Editor Richard Smoley, who watched over the manuscript like a guardian angel, providing direction for improvements with encouragement and wisdom.

Copy editor Judith Stein, capable and compassionate midwife of the final draft, who kept the labor pains to a minimum in the birthing of this book.

# Introduction
## Rediscovering the Shekhinah

Wandering along the California coastline twenty-six years ago, I began to experience the Divine Feminine in the hills, the ocean, and the landscape. A gigantic goddess was calling to me. At first she spoke through sand and rocks, flowers and animals; later she spoke through visions and memories of earlier lives. Still later she spoke through the spirits of the ancestors and Judaism's forgotten women saints and miracle workers.

What was the message? In retrospect it feels as if the first call was to "come home," without many explicit instructions. The visions and past-life memories seemed to be the Lady's way of telling me what and who I had been and could be. Pictures of ancient civilizations and memories of great temples filled my mind with no specific or exclusive ethnoparticularity. Diverse spirit guides provided wisdom that would enable me to help myself and others.

I no longer know how or when I went from a general pantheistic celebration of life to a respiritualized Judaism. It was a gradual process, involving some awakening of the inner music that had always dwelled within. These particular *nitsastot* (sparks of light) were stimulated in Jewish groups, which received me warmly, and whose members also discerned that I had some ritual knowledge and even prayer skills. In 1977 I met Rabbi Zalman Schachter-Shalomi; it would take me a few years to commit myself to rabbinical study with him. Reb Zalman's inspiration and wisdom led me to his other disciples. They in turn led me to a larger piece of my own energy. It was as if I had rediscovered my soul family.

During this same era, I lived at Esalen Institute in Big Sur for three months and experienced a wide variety of therapies and spiritual paths. This was not my first contact with California's magical Central Coast, but it was

1

an important sojourn in the beautiful area that has been my home for the last eighteen years. Northern California also offered numerous opportunities for contact with thinkers and healers trained in the Far East.

While I was always cordially welcomed in these settings, I often felt like the ball in a basketball game in which Hindus, Buddhists, and Native Americans bounced me around and tossed me back into the "Jewish basket." Jewish past-life memories often followed experiences in other sacred settings; it was almost as if the great rebbes were waiting for an atmosphere in which I would open up enough to receive them.

The process of receiving their female counterparts came more easily for me. The search for women teachers had grown like a hunger out of my earlier writings on women in politics and my continuing search for role  models. My path to the Jewish and female bodhisattvas began, like all my inquiries, as the search for data. It took a turn to the esoteric when I realized that their spirits were calling to me. I labeled them Messengers of the Shekhinah and began organizing special meditation circles on their birth dates and *yahrzeits* (death anniversaries) to try to access greater understanding of their lives.

Their message, though arriving through deep emotional and spiritual experience, bore a striking similarity to my earlier political position papers: protect the planet, clean up the environment, stop fighting, take care of kids and old people. At the beginning, the message came with awesome pictures of the potential destruction of the earth and images of my beloved California coming apart. At the same time, the inner voice brought personal directives that changed my life—working differently, caring for the body, and being outdoors. The messages were easy to receive in the clear air on top of Mount Tamalpais. The guides spoke in Berkeley's Tilden Park and appeared in the Sierras. The female voice spoke loudly in Topanga Canyon, issuing instructions shortly before my ordination, and informed my singing at Joshua Tree National Park during the Harmonic Convergence in 1987. It took me into the Anza-Borego oasis and led me into lilac orchards near Julian. The Divine

Presence surrounded me in Hawaii and enveloped me in Israel as well, from the wadis of Ein Gedi to the hiking trails of Gamla.

This voice of the Shekhinah, which I hear on Friday nights after I light my Sabbath candles, has become a constant presence, challenging me to bring it into daily activities and work in the cities. I feel the power of this voice even in Los Angeles, where automobiles and commercialism are destroying the Mother even as talented artists continue to speak for her. Whether the location is secular or sacred, her essence is being trampled by overdevelopment and violence to the earth. There is an ongoing race between creation and destruction.

In the holy city of Jerusalem—where the Shekhinah is immanent at the Western Wall—the struggle is exemplified in the attacks on the "Women of the Wall"—Jewish women who came to pray at the women's side of the wall during the new moon. *Rosh Chodesh* Because the women wore traditional prayer shawls and read from the Torah, they were attacked physically by very Orthodox worshippers who regarded the voice of women in prayer as a violation of tradition. A lengthy lawsuit has ensued. This issue, still to be fully resolved, is one of the many challenges to the return of the Shekhinah to Zion.

Just as I became more connected to Jerusalem, so I became increasingly involved with the Jewish community in the San Francisco Bay area. This era in my life coincided with my daughter's movement from Eastern thought back to Judaism and with my older son's choosing Orthodox Judaism and living in Israel. Members of my extended family also reflected a deep connection with Jewish karma, many emigrating to Israel and becoming committed to the continuation of the culture and religion.

The specific form for my work has been consistently feminist and spiritual, heavily influenced by my years in the women's movement and my training as a social science researcher. The entry into deeper spirituality offered new settings for my progressive voice and rebellious spirit. The trampling of Shekhinah-in-exile was an image I shared with earlier generations of Jewish mystics. In me this image came through as a challenge to Jewish practitioners

3

to recognize that we had been carrying incognito a holy but hidden visitor in our arks for thousands of years. This sense of the Shekhinah also impelled me toward increased study, both formal and informal. Reading extensively, I applied my insights and very limited knowledge to both personal and group experiments with new liturgy and language. Feelings often raced ahead of technique, but I was receiving help from teachers both here and in the other worlds. Often I felt that I knew from another time what was in the text or how to interpret it. This inner knowing, coupled with my own impatience, moved me to teach and spread the word to others, probably long before I was really competent. However, I found colleagues who were also yearning for the Mother's touch. Into my life came Shekhinah poets and songwriters, artists painting on silk, our own Shekhinah videographer/rebbe, and numerous other creative beings who gave us new forms for worshipping the Divine Presence. Linked through invisible cords of spirit, we found each other both at home and in far-off places. As we shared our joy of discovery and our frustration in trying to find support for this work, the search for the Great Jewish Mother was on.

During my wonderful Berkeley years, surrounded and encouraged by many gifted emissaries of Shekhinah, I returned to Jewish studies, which had been the mainstay of my childhood, adolescence, and young adulthood. Although I had been tutored by my grandfather in rural Pennsylvania from the age of three, followed by teen years in the Orthodox Jewish enclave in the Borough Park section of Brooklyn, I had never heard the term *Shekhinah*. Though I attended the prestigious Herzliah School in Manhattan and studied Hebrew as a modern language in both high school and college, this term for the Divine Feminine had never entered my vocabulary. By the time I encountered the Divine Mother, I already had three children and two careers behind me.

Learning why I had never been taught about Shekhinah led me to rediscover how she has unfolded over the centuries, a story I tell in more detail in this book. I realized that when we study the Tanakh (the Hebrew Bible), we do not find the term *Shekhinah* per se, though we may find variations on its root word, which means "to dwell." Hence the term came to mean the indwelling of God, or the Divine who dwells within. *On en a tous...*

To better understand how the term came about, I had to rediscover Onkelos (35–120 C.E.), the intriguing Roman of noble background who embraced Judaism and became one of its foremost explicators. The *Targum Onkelos,* a widely respected Aramaic translation of the Torah used by Middle Eastern Jews for hundred of years, is usually attributed to him, as is the term *Shekhinah* itself. In doing his translation, Onkelos is reputed to have developed and utilized the concept of Shekhinah to avoid any anthropomorphic reference to the deity. In Torah passages that struck him as ascribing human qualities to God, Onkelos would substitute the term *Shekhina*h or sometimes *kavod* (glory) or *memra* (holy word or Logos, which would later come to associate Shekhinah with speech). In effect, *Shekhinah* became a synonym for God. It did not have female gender, even though the word is grammatically feminine. *la chaise, la lune, la joie, la tristesse*

In my studies I also had to return to the world of Midrash, the daily bread of my childhood. My retired grandfather, who studied Gemara and Talmud, had filled my receptive mind with the legends of the Jews. A scholar who visited local communities teaching Torah with me in tow, he probably had no idea he was establishing the template for a future rabbi. As an adult returning to the world of Midrash, I could see how the concept of the Shekhinah reverberated through the literature of the Mishnaic and Talmudic periods to convey the closeness of God, or God's immanence. Developed during the eras of the Tannaim (the early sages of the Mishnaic period, 70–200 C.E.) and the Amorim (teachers who participated in the development of the Talmud, 200–500 C.E.), the genre of literature known as Midrash or Aggadah is commentary on the Torah, the prophets, and the later writings that incorporates such material as stories, dreams, folklore, and homilies. (There are also midrashim on Halakhah, the legal system, but most of the elaboration of Shekhinah's qualities is in the aggadic genre.) The first and most popular midrash was on the Book of Genesis (Bereshit Rabbah), but similar redactions of the oral teachings on the other books of the Bible followed. In these compilations, we see the connection between Shekhinah and the biblical matriarchs and patriarchs as well as the prophets. Shekhinah's presence in all creation and connection with the Ark of the Covenant are also specified. The understanding of Shekhinah as *Ruach ha Kodesh* (Holy Spirit) also became a way of explaining dreams, intuition, vision, and prophecy among gifted humans.

In Midrash and Talmud, Shekhinah continued to be gender neutral or an expression of the male deity, but the concept continued to grow and expand. With the redaction of the Talmud as the major source of explication of Torah and law (completed c. 500 C.E.), new aspects came into the conception of Shekhinah. Even as early as the first exile, to Babylon (586 B.C.E.), Shekhinah had begun to emerge as the suffering Mother of Israel, prefigured by the prophet Jeremiah, who saw a vision of Mother Rachel weeping for the destruction of the temple (Jer. 31:15). A thousand years later, taking on the role of Knesset Yisrael (Community of Israel), Shekhinah, no longer in her Jerusalem Temple, became the traveling guardian and defender of the people of Israel. The sages of the Talmud, believing that Shekhinah was fully present at the beginning in the Garden of Eden, explained that human actions can attract Shekhinah back to earth through charity, prayer, study, and good works. Conversely, they taught, the violence and sins of humanity drive Shekhinah up to the seven heavens, where she can radiate the light and enjoy the company of the angels who are part of her retinue. While I had been resistant to studying Talmud, I found that the ethical concepts associated with Shekhinah (for example, that she leaves when there is violence, pollution, or incest) fit very well with my involvement in peace, civil rights, women's issues, and the environment.

Even in the early literature, Shekhinah hovers over all creation as the guardian of truth and justice. However, the concept becomes more ethnoparticular in assigning Shekhinah's protection to the persecuted people

6

of Israel. What is also apparent in the Talmudic debates is the focus on maintaining the unity of God and taking care not to present Shekhinah as a secondary power with an active role in helping humanity. Despite commitment to that goal, the dialogue often enters uncharted territory in which Shekhinah emerges as a separate voice. While the Talmud did not identify Shekhinah as feminine and continued to present Shekhinah as the expression of the Holy Blessed One, the characteristics attributed to Shekhinah in the rabbinical statements resemble many of the qualities of the ancient goddesses: love, charity, compassion, fairness, equity, healing, justice, power, sharing, and connectedness.

One way the early literature attempted to finesse its portrayals of an active Shekhinah was by associating Shekhinah with the divine light. Volumes have been devoted to this issue, perhaps the best known being Joshua Abelson's monumental work *The Immanence of God in Rabbinical Literature*, in which he characterizes the emerging picture of Shekhinah as a hypostasis, or expression of God. Those views, combined with Judaism's continued taboo on representational art and sculpture, sent Shekhinah to the place of mystical experience and sacred literature. That viewpoint was elaborated by the medieval writers, for whom Shekhinah is the light closest to God and yet is accessible in some way to human consciousness. For me personally, this concept fit in with my meditation practice but did not provide a complete response to the way I was experiencing a more earthy Divine Feminine in my daily life.

The idea of Shekhinah as mother, sister, daughter, and bride emerged with the arrival of the mystical *Sefer Bahir* (Book of Illumination) in medieval Europe, bringing the Divine Feminine into the thinking of the great scholars of that age. Like a shadow figure from behind the curtain, Shekhinah as the Great Lady began to come onto scholarly Judaism's center stage. The ensuing publication of the Zohar (Book of Brilliance) at the end of the thirteenth century, with its bold presentation of the sexual dynamics within the Godhead, set forth very clearly the feminine role in the Tree of Life, although its view was colored by the medieval perspective of the text's writers and commentators. In their formulation, the Shekhinah became the captive princess who has been isolated from her divine partner. Imprisoned or exiled, she is waiting for the knight to rescue her from the forces of evil and restore harmony and balance to the universe. Through prayers, studies, and good deeds the devotee will bring Shekhinah back to her divine partner.

Although this emphasis also did not fit well with a modern feminist outlook, I was captivated by the outrageous creativity of the Zohar. At the Graduate Theological Union in Berkeley in the 1980s, I was introduced to the sacred literature. Dr. Daniel Matt, who is devoting his life and talent to retranslating the Zohar into beautiful English, was the inspired guide who opened up the treasure house of Zohar for me and many others. Study with Rabbi Zalman M. Schachter-Shalomi and other luminous teachers enabled me to continue down the kabbalistic path with a more graceful approach to merging the insights of the past with the enlarged thinking of the present.

I could then appreciate the work of the sixteenth-century Kabbalists of S'fat, whose leaders expanded on the Zohar, bringing profound intuitive and intellectual innovations to the philosophy of Kabbalah. Most of them were Sephardim from Spain and Portugal whose families had endured the suffering of the expulsion and the Inquisition. They were joined by inspired and adventurous teachers from the European and Eastern worlds who shared the dream of returning to Zion and living in spiritual community. S'fat became a kind of utopian Jewish experiment, in which the observance of Jewish law and the leadership of mystics combined to produce a unique society. They seem to me to have had a special connection to the memory of God the Mother. Their poetry, prayers, and visions elevated women on earth, particularly wives and mothers, who they believed served as conduits for the Divine Presence, making it possible for men to receive Shekhinah through marital love and sexuality. But that chivalric process of placing women on a pedestal did not translate into expanded opportunities for the women of their time or of ensuing generations, and their perspective was eclipsed in later centuries, partly because the practices of the S'fat mystics were limited to an elite minority living in dangerous times.

The Shekhinah, always a resilient traveler, made another appearance in the joyous practice of Judaism among the eastern European Chasidim of the eighteenth century. Her role was now seen as the channel to God for the *tsaddik* (saint), her blessings radiating out to women, others lacking scholarly credentials, and beyond to all life forms. While this did not translate into gender equity, it did facilitate the emergence of women saints who embraced and influenced many beings. Although Chasidism was earthy in its outlook, the majority of European Jews could not hold land, so Shekhinah was reenvisioned by the nineteenth-century Haskalah movement as the goal of resettling the Holy Land. This movement, also known as the Jewish Enlightenment, was composed primarily of educated young people living in European countries who longed for a more natural way of life. Their thinking leaned toward a kind of utopian socialism, and they yearned for freedom from anti-Semitism. They believed that creating a Jewish state would provide a more normal future for the Jewish people, and many of them became involved in founding kibbutzim (agricultural communes) and the early socialist political parties in Israel.

While their ideals have been eroded in a modern Israel as it deals with survival as well as environmental and other social issues, many of us still find inspiration all over the Holy Land and in the creative vitality of Israelis. Spiritual pilgrims of all backgrounds still experience the Shekhinah hovering over the one remaining wall of the holy temple, and around the tombs of the great saints who lived on the land. It remains for the future to decide how Shekhinah energy will continue to be expressed and sustained in the Middle East.

With the coming of modernity, the kabbalistic idea that Shekhinah rests on all beings (including stones, plants, animals, and humans, according to the great rabbi Isaac Luria) can come to fruition. Finally, the role of women in creating and expressing their Shekhinah awareness, in their own words, makes it possible for women to project their visions and experience of Shekhinah to a world desperate for rebalancing. In the resurgence of interest in alternative healing modalities and in a broad range of body-work techniques, I feel Shekhinah's presence. In the growing international concern for the environment and the awareness of our planet as a living system, I feel hope for the future. In the connectedness that technology has given us, I see the hand of Shekhinah. I believe that divine energy is inherent in the instant contact we have around the world and can lead us to become a global community. In short, it seems to me that we are capable of creating a future in which Shekhinah is again present here on earth.

May we all be blessed to be participants in that process.

# *I*nvocation
## Appeal to the Matriarchs

We call upon Sarah the priestess, cofounder of Judaism, who gave us the candle-lighting ceremony. Beautiful and holy princess, she celebrated in sacred groves and a simple tent, bringing the light of the Shekhinah wherever she traveled.

Laughing mother of ageless beauty, bless our way.

We call upon Rebekah, who traveled courageously while still a teenager, leaving the shelter of her family to journey toward a new life. Guided to the spiritual path begun by Sarah, she too merited the presence of the clouds of glory and insights into the future of her children.

Courageous mother of difficult choices, bless our way.

We call upon Rachel, whose poignant memory is cherished as the advocate of Israel. Her short life on earth has become a permanent vigil. Forever young, she is always present on the road to exile, watching over her children like the winged Shekhinah.

Romantic and beautiful mother, bless our way.

We call upon Leah, visionary mother of many tribes, progenitor of priests and kings. Like the primal mother of creation, she was blessed with fertility, giving life, giving names, giving nurturance. Great Lady, Mother Binah, Ha'G'veret Ha Elyonah.

Mother of creativity, who sees the future, bless our way.

As we acknowledge the revered Hebrew matriarchs, we also call to our mothers Bilhah and Zilpah, coparents of the emergent Jewish family. We honor your contributions to our spiritual life and include you in our ancestral prayers.

Tribal mothers, bless our way.

We call upon Hagar, mother of the desert life, to whom God's angel spoke directly and who was blessed with the promise of greatness at the Well of Divine Seeing. We ask you to help us heal the wounds between the children of Abraham and mend the torn garment of our interwoven destinies.

Wandering mother, bless our way. *the God who sees me*

Part 1

# Shekhinah in the Tapestry of Time

*For the Shekhinah in the time of Abraham our father is called Sarah and in the time of Isaac our father is called Rebecca and in the time of Jacob our father is called Rachel . . . for Leah is the essence of the "Yovel"* [Jubilee year].

—Rabbi Joseph Gikatilla

*Every single day Rivkah* [Rebekah] *saw the radiance of the Shekhinah in her dwelling and prayed there.*

—Zohar

*Now the Shekhinah never departed from the tent of Leah or the tent of Rachel. . . . The truth is that during the lives of Leah and Rachel the Shekhinah hovered over them.*

—Zohar

*She* [the Shekhinah] *is sometimes called "Daughter" and sometimes "Sister" and here she is called "Mother" and she is indeed all of these.*

—Zohar

Le Bon Dieu
est une
femme
~ Corneille

# Chapter 1

# $\mathcal{G}enesis$
## The Hebrew Matriarchs

The Jewish sages, studying the Torah carefully, found evidence of Shekhinah's presence in many of the stories in Genesis. We are taught that Abraham and Sarah initiated souls by bringing them "under the wings of Shekhinah." For men, the covenant required circumcision and water immersion, or *mikveh*. For women, it required mikveh and possibly some ritual of Sarah's design, which we do not know. (In modern times, there is a long process of study and practice for men and women prior to the actual ceremony.)

The midrashic literature defines Shekhinah's presence as basic to the divine guidance experienced by the founding fathers—Abraham, Isaac, and Jacob—and tells us that the *Ruach ha Kodesh*, or Holy Spirit, animated all the matriarchs as well, giving them prophetic knowledge. The role of the patriarchs, as conduits for the Divine, has been reinforced in later Rabbinic Judaism by the cycle of daily prayer, in which the standing prayer known as Amidah is initiated by calling upon Abraham, Isaac, and Jacob, whose merit facilitates our connection with God. In recent times, the matriarchs have been added to the invocation in the more liberal streams of Judaism. Traditional Jewish prayers for healing *(mi sheberach)* have also been modified to invoke the matriarchs. Traditionally, they are also called upon at burials, in the El Malei Rachamim prayer, when the deceased is a woman. The practice of praying through the merits of the matriarchs is important in the *tekhinot,* European women's prayers written mainly in Yiddish in the eighteenth and nineteenth centuries, suggesting a more continuous and earlier practice.

# Chapter 1

Abraham's power to bless others is also a function of his connection to the Shekhinah, who is Blessing, according to the mystical literature. Abraham is blessed *bakol,* meaning with everything, acquiring land, animals, and wealth wherever he goes. According to Jewish legends, Abraham's son Isaac sees the angels and Shekhinah when he is bound on the sacrificial altar as an offering of his father's profound faith, and he eventually loses his vision because of that encounter. These elements of the legends are consistent with the traditional teaching that we see the Divine Presence as we leave the world. In that same episode, Abraham is supposed to see the Shekhinah when the ram appears as a substitute for Isaac, or possibly when the angel intervenes. Isaac's younger son, Jacob, sustains that connection with Shekhinah and receives the main blessing in place of his older brother, Esau, to become the progenitor of the twelve tribes of Israel. According to Midrash, Jacob's connection with Shekhinah is strongest when he is able to sustain the joy of living; he loses that power when he is depressed, as when he mourns for many years over the presumed death of his favorite son, Joseph. As Jacob prepares to die and blesses his sons (his daughter, Dinah, is not included in the biblical blessings), he intends to share visions of the future with them, but the connection is temporarily disrupted, preventing the prophetic communication. The alignment with Shekhinah is regained when his sons reassure him of their faith by reciting the Sh'ma prayer (the basic one-line statement of faith in Judaism, repeated at every prayer service: "Sh'ma Yisrael Adonai Eloheynu Adonai Echad"—which can be translated, "Listen, all of you who seek the Divine: The Eternal is our God, the Eternal is ONE, there is only One"). Jacob can then leave in peace.

Each of the matriarchs also has her distinctive connection with the Divine Presence. Sarah is portrayed in the aggadic literature as having her own ceremonial tent, where she institutes the candle-lighting ritual for inaugurating the Sabbath, perhaps drawing on much more elaborate temple ceremonies that originated in her native Chaldean background in Ur. In this context, she is the conduit of the light of Shekhinah, which would later be

With flint? How did she light the candles?

ceremonialized in the temple menorah and throughout history in the eternal light lit over the ark in synagogues, called *ner tamid*. Because Sarah is merged with the light of the Shekhinah, the sages say, "Her lamp does not go out at night." In Sarah's ritual tent, which was sheltered by a cloud of glory, the sages tell us that the candles miraculously stayed lit for a whole week. Sarah is the only woman to have a full chapter in the Torah (Chaye Sarah, Gen. 23 and 24), which chronicles her life and death. Enduring and supernal life is attributed to her because of her intimate connection with Shekhinah, who regulates life and death.

Sarah is praised in the Talmud and the Zohar as the woman who "sees" Shekhinah during the famous annunciation scene when three angelic messengers come to predict the birth of Isaac. Her handmaiden, Hagar, who cohabits with Abraham, also has direct connection with divinity and encounters an angel at the well of "the God who Sees." According to Jewish sources, Sarah (whose name means "princess") is blessed with a child in her nineties and experiences many other miraculous events in her heroic journey, including escapes from dangerous and compromising situations. The sages say that her descent into Egypt with Abraham—where her great beauty exposes her to the acquisitive impulses of the Egyptian pharaoh—indicates her ability to deal with negativity and emerge whole, as her life is imbued with divine life. Contemporary feminist scholar Savina Teubal, in tracing the journey of Sarah, portrays her as a priestess who is sought after to perform the *hieros gamos* ceremony, ritually coupling with neighboring kings to assure the fertility of the earth. We also know from the Torah that Sarah resided in sacred groves, among the terebinths of Mamre, suggesting that her ritual work took place at sites already holy to the Canaanite residents of the land. *Memra* is also an attribute of Shekhinah as holy speech. In the Torah, Sarah's special connection to the Divine is exemplified in the deity's instruction to Abraham that in all matters, he "listen to the voice of Sarah."

The miracle of welcoming the Shekhinah in the sacred tent with the candlelighting is maintained by Sarah's daughter-in-law, Rebekah, who keeps the light shining after her marriage to Isaac. She is praised for her generosity to Abraham's servant Eliezer when he comes seeking a bride for Isaac, offering water for Eliezer and his thirsty camels at the communal well. She invites Eliezer to stay with her family, assuring him there is space for him and the animals. In this respect she is very much aligned with her father-in-law, Abraham, who is celebrated for his hospitality. They are precursors to the concept in the Talmud that whoever offers hospitality to a stranger will merit the appearance of Shekhinah. Her connection with water also aligns her with Shekhinah. In the Zohar, the water, a symbol of Shekhinah, rises miraculously to meet Rebekah, enabling her to slake the enormous thirst of the camels. The well, another Shekhinah symbol, also connects her forward in time to her daughter-in-law, Rachel, who meets Jacob at the well, and Tziporah, who meets Moses at the well. The theme is continued through the prophetess Miriam, whose holiness is acknowledged with a miraculous well of water that accompanies the Israelites in the years of wandering in the desert after the Exodus from Egypt.

Rebekah's special qualities as an emissary of the Shekhinah are exhibited in her journey of faith to marry Isaac, the older cousin whom she has never met. When she first sees him, he is out meditating in "the field," another metaphor for Shekhinah. Modestly, she veils herself and alights from her camel to honor him. Their connection is strengthened as she comforts him for the loss of his mother and brings the Shekhinah back into the tent of Sarah. It is said that Isaac, seeing the Shekhinah dwelling in his wife, "embraced faith." Theirs is one of the few successful love stories in the Torah. They have a monogamous marriage, and Isaac demonstrates his devotion to Rebekah by praying on her behalf for children—unlike his son Jacob, who complains when Rachel asks for his help in that regard. There is also no mention of Abraham praying for Sarah to conceive. Later, when Rebekah becomes pregnant, her twins struggle mysteriously in her womb, reflecting the divergent paths they will follow. In Genesis 25:22, she calls on God directly for an understanding of the conflict between the two fetuses. Later commentators suggest that she goes to Abraham or others as intermediaries to ask for divine guidance, but the Torah text itself states that she inquires directly of God. When the twins as men take different paths, she intervenes to guarantee that her younger son, Jacob, receive the main blessing from his father, Isaac. This is attributed, in the legends, to premonitory knowledge from her connection with Shekhinah, informing her that Jacob is destined to become the spiritual leader of the people of Israel.

The matriarch Rachel is introduced to us in the Torah as a beautiful shepherdess bringing her herd to the well, where she has her first meeting with her cousin Jacob, a dramatic example of love at first sight. Jacob, a simple man not known for strength, is empowered to remove the stone from the well. The romance of Jacob and Rachel thus begins like the Arthurian legend in which the hero must pull the sword from the stone. Their initially highly romantic relationship ultimately descends into a complex family drama full of frustration and jealousy. Rachel's inability to have children for some years undermines her satisfaction with life, despite Jacob's great love for her. The Genesis narrative gives us a picture of a competitive extended family, caught in a historical shift from matrilocal to patriarchal, in which the sexual favors of Jacob become a source of tension between Rachel and her sister, Leah, and the two additional co-wives, Bilhah and Zilpah, because their status depends on providing sons to the patriarch. Rachel, the beloved wife, dies young giving birth to her second son, Benjamin, and becomes a kind of patron saint for Jewish women with fertility challenges. The Jewish mystics transform her in death from the beautiful earthly wife into the Lower Shekhinah who watches over the people of Israel. She becomes associated with the realm of Malkhut, the attribute located at the base of the Tree of Life (see chapter 7, Kabbalah: The Feminine on the Tree of Life). Buried at a crossroads, Rachel assumes the eternal role of pleading directly to God on behalf of the exiled Israelites. She represents Shekhinah watching over the earth and all its inhabitants. Described by the prophet Jeremiah as "weeping in Ramah for the return of her children to the land," she becomes the people's guardian spirit.

While this portrait of Rachel was already present in the prophetic era, it was elaborated considerably in the mystical literature.

The midrashic literature describes the sister matriarchs, Leah and Rachel, as being able to see the future, like priests and prophets, whose intuition is drawn from Shekhinah. Leah is introduced in the Torah as having weak eyes (or perhaps soft or tender). According to the medieval commentator Rashi, this difficulty was the result of her weeping over her presumed destiny to be married to Jacob's brother Esau, who was known to be a rough and insensitive fellow. Other commentaries say she was able to see the future suffering of the children of Israel and wept for them. Some modern commentators see the power of her tears as transforming her fate; and there has been more focus in modern Kabbalah, especially in the writings of Moshe Idel, on weeping as a mystical practice.

In the biblical story, Jacob, who was already in love with Rachel, acquires a heavily veiled Leah as his first wife through the deception of their crafty father, Laban. The Zohar cites the participation of Rachel in this drama, crediting her with not wanting to see her older sister shamed. Leah subsequently gives birth to six sons and a daughter, fulfilling her kabbalistic role as Great Mother, in which each of her children represents one of the seven lower Sephirot, or embodiments of the divine attributes on the Tree of Life. In the Torah, she is the great name-giver. According to the Zohar, her capacity to name her numerous children appropriately is inspired by the Shekhinah, which enables her to "see into" their character. Leah, the senior matriarch, whose son Judah became the progenitor of the main surviving tribe of Israel, is buried with Jacob in the cave of the Machpelah in Hebron with the other ancestors.

The great sage Rabbi Shimon Bar Yochai, who lived in the second century, warned against considering these narratives in Genesis as just stories and urged a deeper analysis of their meaning. The midrashic and mystical literature that followed laid the groundwork for a metaphorical understanding of the archetypal energies represented by these ancestral personalities, each with some special destiny to fulfill. In that context, the Zohar's presentation of Leah and Rachel as twin aspects, or different manifestations, of Shekhinah energy on the Tree of Life provides an alternate understanding of the painful romantic triangle. The Zohar regards Leah's role as founder of the tribes and mother of future leaders as representing the Upper Mother, Binah, who gives birth to planets and stars. In fact, the Zohar states that Jacob did not "hate" Leah as the text implies, but felt a strangeness with her as he might in coupling with his mother! Her reunification with Rachel, the daughter or Lower Mother, who protects planet earth, is essential to the cosmic plan, as is the marriage with the Sephira of Tiferet, represented by Jacob, in the center of the Tree. He is the divine masculine consort to Malkhut, the Divine Feminine—or Shekhinah—at the base of the Tree of Life.

The Shekhinah also figures prominently in midrashim on the sisters' sex life with Jacob. In the legends, the Shekhinah rests over the tent of the wife he will sleep with that night, reminiscent of the clouds of glory in Exodus. After Rachel's death, the cloud moves to her co-wife, Bilhah. In the mystical tradition, Bilhah and Zilpah are the "handmaidens" of Shekhinah, almost like the two cherubs who flank the Ark of the Covenant. In mystical thought, Rachel and Leah endure as twin aspects of Shekhinah or embodiments of the Divine Presence. Because of the importance of the sisters, the Jewish midnight prayers enunciated on behalf of the planet, called *tikkun chatzot,* are directed to both. That concept leads to regarding women—particularly mothers—as the closest representation of the Divine Mother we can know in earthly form. While the Midrash gives us hints about the spiritual power of the matriarchs, we do not know the specific nature of their practices. New midrashim by women scholars and fiction by writers like Anita Diamante (*The Red Tent*) help keep the mystery alive.

# Meditation

## Remembering the Matriarchs

It is midnight. I look out my window, and I know that this radiant moon that shines down on me was there for my mother, and my grandmothers, and my great-grandmothers, that we all understand our special relationship to the moon. We understand why the great Jewish mystics prayed and meditated and traveled through space between midnight and five AM. They taught that this was a special time when God's compassion on the world was more open, more available; and that in this time of willingness in the heavens above, if we down below would pray, we could enlist divine assistance for all life and the planet itself.

Tikkun chatzot are prayers designed to appeal for the health of the planet, prayers that bring an awareness of just how endangered this earth is. We send petitions addressed to the matriarchs, to Leah, representing the Upper Shekhinah in the higher realms, in the Sephira of Binah, and to Rachel, representing the Lower Shekhinah connected with us here on earth. Most of us don't know the words of these prayers, and even those of us who know them tend to see them as very long and complex. So we look for a direct route to the Creator, expressing ourselves through our mothers and our grandmothers and our great-grandmothers.

Let us start with our own families. We picture our mother, perhaps an image of her when she was young and lovely and hopeful and about to give birth to us. We call her in, and we ask her, "Dear one, how did you experience the Divine Presence? What gave you faith and courage and hope, and enough strength to bring us forth? For even in your time, there were so many problems in the world. And we thank you for giving us the gift of life, the most precious gift that anyone could receive. We ask you to help us, whether you're in this world or the other world, to become the people that we were destined to be." We ask for help in visualizing our grandmothers, even if we didn't know them both, along with their families, their communities, the places they came from, and the struggles they endured to create a better life for their children. We try to imagine how they spoke to the Shekhinah, how they imagined the Divine Presence. If we go a bit further back, we ask for memory of our great-grandmothers, even if we never saw them, even if we have no photographs of them. We ask to know them inside ourselves and to feel their love and their longing to be in connection with the innermost expression of the Divine One.

Now we want to surround these women from our extended families with great souls, probably from other lineages and other backgrounds. So many of us have been blessed by teachers and saints from other parts of the world who have come to expand our awareness. So if you have teachers and guides that speak to you in some way, place them around your own family, and create a circle of holy beings surrounding and protecting them, and likewise surrounding you. Place yourself in the middle of the circle so that you feel all this radiance. Once you are in the center of the circle, listen, listen for the voices of your ancestors. Listen for the wisdom of the matriarchs.

Now breathe with me, intentionally. Continue breathing and feeling your resonance with all the matriarchal souls around you. And let your breath join the breath of the larger circle, extending out and merging with the breath of Shekhinah.

*And the Lord went before them by day, in a pillar of cloud to lead their way, and by night in a pillar of fire to give them light to travel day and night. The pillar of cloud by day and the pillar of fire by night did not leave them.*

—Exodus

*The Shekhinah was accompanied by all the clouds of glory, and when it journeyed the Israelites took up their march. . . . And when the Shekhinah ascended the cloud also ascended.*

—Zohar

*Let them build me a sanctuary and I will live among and within them.*

—Exodus

*And I will set my tabernacle among you. "My tabernacle" means the Shekhinah.*

—Zohar

# Chapter 2

# *The Desert Experience*
## Divine Presence in Nature

*T*he Book of Exodus is replete with references to the presence of Shekhinah. She manifests in the water of the Red Sea and in Miriam's well; in the air as the clouds of glory; in fire as the pillar of fire; and on the earth, where the Israelites gather the miraculous manna. We can clearly see the direct connection to the natural elements. In effect, the long trek through the Sinai Desert is preparing the people for their dramatic encounters with divinity; they are traveling together on an extended vision quest. First is the dramatic escape of the Israelite slaves from the pursuing Egyptian army across a miraculously divided sea. Numerous legends allude to visions of Shekhinah during that dramatic crossing, raising the experience of the simplest of women workers to the level of the prophets. Thus, metaphorically, the Israelites journey through the watery womb of the Great Mother and emerge reborn on dry land. The Torah describes how they are saved by the cloud of Shekhinah placed between the Hebrews and the Egyptians, so that the attackers are in the dark and the pursued are in the light. The all-powerful protective Mother destroys the Egyptian pursuers, fulfilling her assigned role as mobilizer of the armies of God and punisher of the wicked. Here, she is Shekhinah, as she would later be described kabbalistically, in the power emanation called Gevurah, which we find on the Tree of Life. Also called Din (law and judgment), it is a feminine attribute that embodies the energies of power and discernment, as well as the establishment and maintenance of appropriate boundaries. That view of Shekhinah as punishing the wicked is present in early rabbinic literature even before it became part of the later kabbalistic model. This fiercer countenance of the Shekhinah is similar to the goddess Kali, who destroys illusions and negativity in Hindu tradition.

On dry land, the children of Israel are guided during the day by seven clouds of glory *(anan ha kavod)* and at night by a pillar of fire *(amud ha esh)* that warms them and lights their way. The Torah tells us that their travel depends on the positioning of the clouds. When the clouds rest on the Holy Ark, the dwelling place of Shekhinah, the people camp. When the clouds lift up, they move on. In effect, the clouds of Shekhinah guide them through the desert by day, and the fire of Shekhinah warms and illuminates them at night, providing a constant protective presence in their journey toward higher consciousness.

As they begin to travel, without conventional sources of food and water, their physical needs are supplied in miraculous manner. The Israelites always have enough water provided from the well of Miriam, a beehive-shaped stone well that rolls along with them. Designed by the Creator in advance recognition of the role of Miriam, this well is said to have been created on the sixth day of creation prior to the Sabbath. The people are fed by the emergence of the manna, a fluffy white substance that could be infused with one's culinary desires—a sort of spiritual tofu. There is always enough for everyone. In fact, a kind of mystic socialism prevails in which those who gather more find their portion reduced, while those who do not gather much find their share amplified. This miracle food/manna that they gather from the earth is labeled by some commentators as *ziv ha Shekhinah* (the light of the Divine Presence). This suggests that in the desert, the Hebrews were eating no ordinary food, but the light of the Shekhinah! The manna, like the well of the prophetess Miriam, is also attributed to the sixth day of creation prior to the Sabbath.

Thus the Israelites are blessed with a variety of miracles leading up to the giving of the Ten Commandments at Mount Sinai and are constantly reminded of the Divine Presence in the natural environment. In addition to all these manifestations of God's protection, there is the blessing of the three great leaders Moses, Aaron, and Miriam, who communicate with the Holy Spirit. Moses, considered the greatest of the Hebrew prophets, enters the cloud of Shekhinah and speaks directly with the Divine Presence under the cherubim that cover the ark with their vast wings. Aaron, designated by the Creator as chief ritualist, deals with the incense and sacrifices that later become the hallmark of Shekhinah's presence in the Jerusalem Temple. Shekhinah's cloud is said to hover over him, and he is praised by the commentators as the mediating force or peacemaker among the people. Miriam, who is designated as prophetess in the Torah, is considered a "pneumatic," the one who leads through the voice and the breath. Also described as the holy dancer and singer in Exodus, she leads the women in ecstatic praise of the deliverance from Egypt.

Even before the Hebrew slaves go free, the midrash speaks of the role of Shekhinah in giving birth to the Exodus generation—those who would go from bondage to freedom. We are told that the women went out to the fields where their husbands were working and seduced them into having sexual relations outdoors, overcoming their usual modesty to create the next generation. The presence of Shekhinah is thus portrayed as being closer or more accessible out of doors, as with Moses's encounter with the burning bush, and connects with much later kabbalistic teaching that to experience Shekhinah, one need only go into an apple orchard in bloom and breathe! Prominent among the resulting generation of "Shekhinah babies" is the divine child Moses, whose birth is predicted by his sister, Miriam the prophetess—a most powerful messenger of the Shekhinah. Because of Pharaoh's edict to kill all the boy babies, Moses's father, Amram, a leader in his tribe, had divorced his wife, Yocheved, and other men had followed suit. Miriam, still a child, foresees the birth of the future redeemer and challenges her father's decision. The parents are reunited, and the midrash tells us that Shekhinah was present in the bed of Amram and Yocheved when they conceived Moses. In the Torah, Yocheved—the mother of Moses, Aaron, and Miriam—is referred to as Bat Ha-Levi. While she is indeed the daughter of

Chapter 2

Levi, son of Jacob and leader of one of the twelve tribes, Bat-Ha-Levi is also one of the Zohar's code names for Shekhinah. When this holy woman/midwife gives birth to her child, without labor pains, baby Moses's presence fills the house with light.

Other legends detail the miraculous birth and infancy of baby Moses, a child of the light who is said to have been already circumcised at birth and to have begun to speak at three months old. Protected by the Divine Mother, he radiates light from his little floating ark onto the Egyptian princess who rescues him. She becomes Bat-Ya (daughter of God) and is instantly healed of her skin disease by the light of Shekhinah that surrounds the holy child. She is also said to have a supernatural death, ascending directly to heaven, where she rejoices with the Hebrew matriarchs. The frescoes excavated from the third-century c.e. synagogue in Dura-Europos (modern Syria) portray the scene of Pharaoh's daughter plucking the Hebrew child from the reeds. Watching over the baby Moses like a Greco-Roman goddess is a beautiful nude figure, which in *The Hebrew Goddess*, Raphael Patai considered to be Shekhinah.

As Moses grows up in the Egyptian palace, he is probably trained in the cult of Isis by his adoptive royal mother. According to the biblical narrative, Moses is nursed by his natural mother, Yocheved, who then instructs him secretly in the Jewish traditions. Later in life, Moses is portrayed in the commentaries as Ish Ha Elohim (consort of God/dess), who becomes inseparable from the Divine Presence. Of all the Hebrew prophets, only Moses has a face-to-face—or face-to-back—encounter with God. When Moses asks to see God, he is told that he cannot see the deity and live, so God passes before him as he stands inside the cleft of a rock, able to see only God's back. Moses dies with the kiss of the Shekhinah, as do his siblings. But only he is carried aloft to an unknown burial place on the wings of the Shekhinah, who descends in birdlike form to carry him to his final and mysterious resting place.

The Midrash and the Zohar establish Moses's spiritual/erotic relationship to Shekhinah both directly and indirectly. The latter emerges through stories about the celibacy practiced by Moses in his later years, when he separates himself from his wife, Tziporah, after they have had children, so he can be constantly available to the Shekhinah to enter and inspire him. That issue of Moses's celibacy is related to an incident in the Torah (Numbers 1211–16) in which Moses's siblings—Miriam the prophetess and Aaron the high priest—challenge Moses's leadership. Some interpreters connect this incident to the celibacy issue, suggesting that the criticism that leads to Miriam's punishment with leprosy is not related to the race of Moses's Midianite wife, Tziporah, as a simple reading would imply. Instead, the issue is Miriam's criticism of Moses's abstention from marital relations and her suggestion that contact with their respective partners does not make them less accessible to Ruach ha Kodesh. Often translated as "Holy Spirit," Ruach ha Kodesh is what imparts prophetic insight; it is also another frequently used term for Shekhinah.

The legendary notion of Moses as consort of Shekhinah emerges from a review of the many commentaries on Moses, as well as the biblical story in which his mother sets him adrift on the Nile in a small ark in the hope of saving his life. In this story he is reminiscent of the Egyptian god Horus, which suggests that the Moses myth is grounded in a larger, older Middle Eastern context. The Jewish contribution to the archetypal story of the Hero's Journey is of the emergent ethical-political-religious leader who guides his followers to the place and time where the whole group's connection with the Divine becomes activated in a shared spiritual epiphany. At Mount Sinai, Moses brings the Israelites to an area that he had explored earlier, during his apprenticeship with Jethro, the priest of Midian, his mentor and father-in-law. It was during his early adulthood in this same area of the Sinai Desert that Moses encounters the Shekhinah in the burning bush. The Rabbis ask why God chooses the lowly thorn bush—perhaps a cactus, like the flaming red ocotillo—as the vehicle for Moses's initiation. They answer that it is "to remind us that the Shekhinah is present in everything, including the stones and the plants. There is nowhere on Earth devoid of Her presence" (Talmud

Shabbat 67a). Much later, in the sixteenth century, the great mystic Rabbi Isaac Luria would remind us that Shekhinah is present in *ha domeh* (the stones), *ha stameach* (the plants), *ha b'heimah* (the living creatures), and *ha 'm'dabeyr* (those who speak, that is, humankind).

Despite that belief in the ubiquitous nature of God's presence, the wandering Israelites proceed to build an ark to house the Shekhinah. The challenge of being in connection with an abstract, formless God, despite many visible miracles and the voice of the prophet Moses, is ongoing. The Torah describes it in its negative form as the construction of the golden calf after Moses does not descend from the mountain when expected. The challenge is resolved positively in the building of the beautiful Mishkan or Tabernacle, which becomes Shekhinah's dwelling place on earth. Both *Mishkan* and *Shekhinah* are rooted in the Hebrew term for dwelling, *lishkon*. The wandering and as-yet-homeless Israelites have difficulty accepting a deity who is also a wanderer. That deep longing for divine revelation in the material world—which they must have encountered in the gods of Egypt—is reflected in the people's ardent participation in the building of the Mishkan. The Torah relates how everyone comes forward with gifts, to the point that Moses is overwhelmed by the offerings. Women and men, common folk and tribal leaders all present the best of what they have. The sanctuary gleams with gold and silver, copper, and brass. It is embellished with curtains of woven and dyed goat hair (the talent of women weavers) and the skins of valued marine mammals. There is color and form, beauty and opulence to accompany them on their challenging entry into the land. The people secure their sought-after edifice, their portable temple, which they can enclose in the tent of meeting that miraculously holds them all.

The Mishkan travels with the people of Israel to the Promised Land, providing the needed protection of the Divine as they struggle with a new environment and often-hostile neighbors. The role and location of the ark and the Mishkan continue to be critical elements in the spiritual life of Israel over the centuries. These elements also become a feature in Israel's later military and political struggles, when the ark is brought out for protection during wars.

Later legends speculate on how God shrinks in size to fit into the Mishkan and provide a gathering place for ceremonies. Receiving divine instructions and specifications through Moses, the people embellish their *ohel moed,* or tent of meeting, with all manner of skins and fabrics. Women embroider designs of rich color full of nature symbols, including palms and pomegranates, which were sacred to the goddess in earlier Middle Eastern cultures. The Mishkan, this sanctuary or holy dwelling, then becomes the meeting place for Shekhinah and her consort lover YHVH, who descends nightly to make love to her. Through this hieros gamos, or sacred marriage, the earth is restored each day and the life of the people directed and guaranteed. Various rabbinical parables talk about the ability of the Ark of the Covenant, a box less than five feet long, to contain the presence of the Divine! For Shekhinah is not only able to be in all places at all times, but can also constrict herself to the small space between the two cherubim who span the ark, where God converses with and through Moses.

At the doorway of the tent sits a group of mysterious women who provide some important service for the group's ceremonial life. We don't really know whether they are priestesses, oracles, or handmaidens of Shekhinah. The Zohar implies that the *petach ohel moed,* the opening to the tent of meeting, is another euphemism for the Divine Feminine—in effect, the sacred vaginal opening reminiscent of the caves of the goddess in prehistoric Europe. Perhaps these women are guardians who ensure that one's entry is appropriate. Into this holy tent come not only Moses and Aaron, not only priests and Levites, but also, according to the legends, all six hundred thousand male souls, plus who knows how many women and children, on the desert journey! Here again is proof of God's willingness to contract and expand on our behalf. The grateful people do their share, participating in the building and embellishment of the sanctuary. Some have higher levels of skill, being imbued with *chochmat ha lev,* or wisdom of the heart, and are

31

# Chapter 2

called upon as holy artisans. But all come forward in what may have been the first temple-building fund, donating according to their means and skills. In fact, they are so generous (especially the women) that the contributions exceed the need, presenting Moses with a kind of crisis. The relevant chapters of the Torah describe in great detail the exact nature of the gifts brought forward and the more lavish contributions of the princes of the tribes.

It has always been interesting to speculate on how the fleeing slaves managed to accrue those riches. The Torah tells us that Jewish women borrowed jewels and other precious items from their *shekheinot* (neighbors) in Egypt and then left with the liberated items. I prefer an interpretation suggesting that the Jewish and Egyptian women shared close relationships based on the awareness of their understanding of the Divine Feminine. When it came time to leave, the Jewish women asked for a blessing for their journey and for their children in the form of precious stones, representing the Shekhinah.

Despite the democracy of giving, there are important taboos as to who may approach the altar. Warnings as to how interactions with the divine energy influenced by personal ego can result in obliteration are implied in the case of Aaron's sons—the younger priests Nadav and Avihu—who are consumed by a fire that descends when they enthusiastically enter the sacred area with "strange or foreign fire." Is this the destroying aspect of the Shekhinah, taking them back? The commentaries portray the two young men as egotistical and competitive with their father. Later in the Talmud, ego and self-importance are declared anathema to the presence of Shekhinah.

After the death of Miriam the prophetess and the drying up of the feminine waters, the narrative gets caught up with protest and rebellion, with punishment for those who go off the path. Without the security of the water from Miriam's miraculous well, the people become more and more obstreperous. They push Moses to the point where he disobeys the divine instructions. Is this a demonstration of the loss of the feminine softness of God, represented by the flowing waters associated with Miriam? Over and over

again, no matter how many miracles, no matter how much divine intervention on their behalf, the group always backslides into complaints about
physical conditions and attacks on the leadership of Moses. Is the Torah
teaching us something about the human condition? Fed with the miraculous manna, the Israelites reject spiritual vegetarianism and manage to ex-
tract quails from the irritated deity. God fights their wars and makes sure
their clothes and shoes never wear out. But the moment there is a lack of
basics, the people accuse Moses of bringing them to the desert to die.

From the building of the golden calf and the shattering of the first set of
tablets, the codification of practice takes over in the Torah text. Hints of
Shekhinah's intervention in history become part of the collective memory
as the emphasis moves to the rules for the celebration of holidays and regu-
lation of communal religious life. The deity sees that humans need rules
and proceeds to dish out a long list of do's and don'ts. We are leaving our
innocent state in the desert, just as we once left our innocent time in the
garden. The small statue of the sacred calf, so widespread in the Middle East
that thousands of them have been unearthed in Israel, was normally a be-
nign symbol of other gods and goddesses. In Jewish thought, the golden calf
came to represent a fall, the return to materialism and licentiousness. Like
the Tower of Babel, it becomes recurring proof that humankind always goes
off the path, even when the group has been the beneficiary of divine guidance in its daily life. There is a beautiful midrash to the effect that there was
a prior set of tablets that was not rectilinear but designed in spiraling shapes,
from swirling energies more typical of the feminine. The implication is that
in the world to come, we will be able to relinquish the harder black-and-
white language of the Decalogue tablets and return to an earlier code, presented in rounder forms.

# Meditation

## Ruach Hamidbar (Spirit of the Desert)

You are going out in the desert, on an encampment with a wonderful group. You decide what to bring with you: some water and light food, your drums or other musical instruments, perhaps a lightweight tent and an air mattress.

You are going to a sacred spot. You have strong leaders who know the way, who help you set out with confidence and keep to a pace that is just right. Everyone seems to be in synchrony.

You find yourself under a brilliant full moon; it is lighting up the still-warm sand. The temperature is perfect: it is pleasant and warm, with a subtle night-time breeze that carries the scent of flowers in bloom and the spirit of the Shekhinah.

You come to an oasis of date palms. There is a spring of clear water, suitable for drinking, and a fire pit for the ubiquitous amud ha esh, the pillar of fire that will warm the night.

There are delicate oval-shaped clouds above you in the starry night sky, the miraculous seven clouds of glory, reminding you of Shekhinah's protective presence.

Musicians begin drumming and singing. All join in.

You begin to feel the blessing of the gathering, of a presence within and beyond yourself. You feel at one with everyone and everything. You want to lie down in the sand and become one with the Divine Presence.

From that consciousness, you ask the holy Mother to send you a vision . . . or a message. . . . It can be sound or fragrance, visual or tactile.

Allow yourself to sink into this divine pleasure, and be the recipient.

*She* [Asherah] *is worshipped on any green tree, on any high hill.*

—Jeremiah

*They bring out the Asherah from the house of the Lord.*

—II Kings

*May you be blessed by Yahweh and his Asherah.*

—Kuntillet Ajrud excavation, northeast Sinai

*The name Asherah was removed from Shekhinah so that the [Canaanite]* *... goddess would not be empowered by the invocation of that name.*

—Zohar

# Chapter 3

# *Canaan*

## Encountering the Pagan Past

The Hebrew people enter the land, begin to settle down, and go through their dance of attraction–repulsion with their neighbors. Their connection with the rituals of their goddess-worshipping Canaanite neighbors symbolizes the powerful drama going on in the evolving Israelite psyche. They are being guided by powerful and prophetic leaders toward worship of the more abstract monotheistic version of the cloud-rider God, but they are still tied to the earth.

Is the attraction to pagan practice a reflection of their yearning for nature and freedom? Are the Israelite men being seduced by the freer sexual practices of the Canaanite people, who may still have been enacting the ritual of sacred marriage to ensure the earth's fertility? The practice of "sacred prostitution" was known and available to Jewish men, as cited in the story of Judah and Tamar (Gen. 38:6–30). Are they having difficulty letting go of the belief in God as the fruitful mother who brings forth the bounty of the earth and provides for her children? While that quality has been transposed to the masculine deity, Asherah still speaks to the need for a household goddess who is close to humans in their daily lives.

Excavations in northern Israel attest to the presence of small clay figurines of Asherah—usually holding her breasts—for hundreds of years. The ubiquitous Canaanite goddess, known as Mother of the Sea and associated with the Tree of Life, was the chief matriarch of the Ugaritic pantheon and wife of the chief god, known as El. In that capacity, Asherah gives birth to the seventy gods and goddesses. The best known of her progeny are Anat, the fierce warrior goddess, and Baal, the cloud-rider god, with whom the

37

Israelites are often in conflict. The Torah frequently cites their continued fascination with Baal, and the prophets repeatedly attack the continued worship of Asherah on the *bamot* (altars on high hills) and even in the temple itself.

Whatever role these goddess energies may have played in the formative lives of the Jewish matriarchs, aggadic tradition portrays the early Israelite women as having embraced the Mosaic faith more easily than men. The commentaries on Exodus praise women for refusing to contribute their jewelry to the construction of the golden calf. Did the women know that the old religion was weakening from outside attacks or no longer viable, and that they needed to change? Or did they take the goddess practices underground, using them during childbirth, illness, and death? Perhaps they kept them quietly at home, near the cooking hearth, where thousands of Asherah figurines have been found in archeological digs all over Israel, covering an extended span of Israelite history.

All the Hebrew matriarchs came from goddess-worshipping cultures. Sarah is from the Chaldean/Sumerian culture, with its veneration of the goddess Inanna. Rebekah is described as coming from a family of pagan worshippers. We know from the Torah that Rebekah's brother, Laban, consults the *teraphim* (idols) for guidance. Laban, who is Rachel and Leah's father, is a devotee of the pagan path. His name means "white" or "moonlike" (*levanah*, "moon"). Abraham's father is called *Terach*, a name connected to another word for moon, *yorayach*. Both names may archetypally represent the old Babylonian connection to the early moon god Sin, part of the pantheon estimated to date to 12,000 B.C.E. or earlier. At the Hazor excavation in northern Israel, with its rich history dating back to the Bronze and Iron Ages, Yigael Yadin unearthed the famous Bronze Age stele in which hands are upraised in blessing or worship toward a crescent and full moon.

Rebekah leaves this family of pre-patriarchal origin to marry Isaac, but she is undoubtedly familiar with the old practices. She is portrayed in Genesis 27:46 as unhappy about the possibility of her sons marrying local Hittite women and bringing their spiritual practices home. Having been raised in a matrifocal home, her fear of "intermarriage" may be more connected with loneliness for the customs of her culture than an objection to the local people. In fact, Esau, Jacob's twin brother, takes a third wife from the family of Ishmael (Hagar and Abraham's son), who is more acceptable to Isaac and Rebekah.

The second foremother of Judaism was part of Abraham's family of origin, which remained in an area still devoted to the many gods worshipped by Abraham's father, Terach, the creator of idols. Just as Abraham's servant Eliezer is sent back to the old homestead to bring Isaac a bride from the extended family, Jacob is directed to the family of Rebekah's origin when he must flee from home. In fact, the ploy Rebekah supposedly uses is the need for Jacob to go and find a bride (Gen. 28:1–3). While the extended family may still be pagan—and prove to be untrustworthy and exploitative, as in the case of Laban—they are blood relatives.

Jacob's wives, Rachel and Leah, as Laban's daughters, are also familiar with these practices; the matriarch Rachel "steals" the teraphim when Jacob's family leaves her family compound for good. According to some commentators, this is to keep her father from idol worship. Others suggest that her retention of the totemic items is a guarantee of her leadership as the youngest in the family. In Genesis 31, Laban comes looking for the idols, and Rachel hides them beneath her, pleading menstruation to keep from standing in honor of her father. But she suffers from her connection with the pagan figures and ultimately dies as a result of Jacob having sworn that the one who stole the statues will be punished with death.

The matriarch Leah names the children of her handmaiden, Zilpah, for the Ugaritic gods Gad and Asher. Although the Biblical text (Genesis 30:9–14) denotes the Hebrew derivations, this could have been a recognition and honoring of Zilpah's roots.

Despite their upbringing, the matriarchs Sarah, Rebekah, Rachel, and Leah seem ready to embrace the new religion and "take it on the road."

# Chapter 3

While this appears to be a paradox, perhaps it is because the goddess worship, the prevailing faith for centuries, has already been attacked and lost some of its power. Perhaps the practices have become adulterated or corrupted; and these women, with their enhanced vision, feel it is time to move on to a new and more abstract faith. Some contemporary feminists have attacked Judaism as the reason for the downfall of the goddess, but in fact goddess worship was already weakened when the new faith came on the scene.

The co-wives of the patriarchs—including Hagar, Bilhah, and Zilpah—also come from goddess-worshipping cultures. The Torah and the commentaries identify Hagar as Egyptian (possibly a princess and a priestess), and the other two wives are probably from the surrounding culture and may have embraced monotheism as part of their connection with the founding family. The significant Jewish leaders for many generations to come marry women who have been trained in worship of the goddess, including Moses's wife, Tziporah, who is the daughter of Jethro, priest of Midian; and Joseph's wife, Asnath, daughter of Potiphar, priest of On.

The Messianic lineage is established by the marriage between Boaz, of the tribe of Judah, and Ruth, the Moabite heroine who adopts Judaism. Three great prophets, Jeremiah, Ezekiel, and Huldah, are considered descendants of Rahab—the innkeeper and sacred prostitute of Jericho who hides the Israelite spies—from her legendary marriage with Joshua, the leader of Israel, who follows Moses. Other sources align Rahab with Caleb ben Yefuneh, one of the scouts who gives a good report of the land. Later, during the monarchy, Kings David and Solomon take numerous "foreign" wives, which always has the potential for bringing in goddess worship. That is certainly the case in the history of northern Israel, where Queen Maacah and Jezebel were known devotees of the Canaanite goddesses. The prophet Elijah's famous battle with the prophets of Baal and Asherah on Mount Carmel (I Kings 18) is fundamental to the Jezebel story. Interestingly, Elijah kills the prophets of Baal, but there is no mention of a similar dire fate for the prophets of Asherah.

# Canaan

Various incidents in the Torah deal with the Israelites' fatal attraction for pagan festivities. The story of Zimri and Cuzbi portrayed in Numbers 25:14–16 is one of the most dramatic. The Jewish tribal prince Zimri flaunts his relationship with a Canaanite princess/priestess and has sex with her in the Jewish camp. During the act, they are both speared to death by Pinchas, a zealous Hebrew priest, who is credited with saving the Israelite camp from a "plague" brought on by Zimri's actions. Legends tell us it was part of a plot concocted by foreign shamans to divert the Jews from the true path. In fact, the commentators say that Cuzbi, the daughter of the chieftain, had her eye on Moses as the real prize. The protagonists in the ongoing dance with the pagans are almost always men, who probably had greater freedom of movement than the women. They are supposedly drawn to the sexual ceremonies of the surrounding peoples, whose practices are free of the demanding Mosaic code. There are suggestions of wild bacchanalian celebrations and possibly promiscuity and group sex. How much of this is true and how much a projection onto rituals celebrating the sacred marriage and the rites of "sacred prostitution," we do not know. We have only one biblical story of a woman possibly involved with, or curious about, her Canaanite neighbors. Dinah, the daughter of Leah and Jacob, "goes out to see the women of the land," which may suggest a visit during some kind of celebration, or possibly just a friendly visit. She is subsequently raped or seduced by the local prince of Shechem. The medieval commentator Rashi projects flirtatious behavior on her part, suggesting that her subsequent rape was induced by her improper behavior. The liaison leads to an attack on the men of Shechem by Dinah's brothers while the local males are recovering from the circumcision ritual that has been requested as part of an agreement for Shechem to marry Dinah. Her brothers are supposedly defending Dinah's honor, but she is never heard from again in the Torah text. Various commentaries have her living out her days in the home of her brother Shimon; others say that her daughter from the liaison with Shechem is saved by the patriarch Jacob, adopted by the Egyptian priest Potiphar, and named Asnath; and that the child of Dinah's encounter with Shechem ultimately marries Joseph in Egypt, who recognizes her origins by an amulet that Jacob placed around her neck!

Contemporary writers who have studied the Torah text offer alternative explanations. In his book *And They Took Them Wives*, David Bakan makes the case for an ongoing matrifocal spirituality that drew on the Asherah/ Astarte practices. Savina Teuval makes a powerful case for Sarah as priestess, reinterpreting the journeys of Abraham and Sarah. As noted earlier, we know from the Torah that Sarah spent time in the terebinths of Mamre, groves of trees possibly sacred to the goddess. Teuval suggests that Sarah, as traveling priestess/princess, would have been sought out by the neighboring kings to enact the sacred marriage to guarantee the abundance of the earth.

The most interesting literature supporting these possibilities is Raphael Patai's *The Hebrew Goddess*, first published in 1967. His research documented the existence of Asherah worship for hundreds of years while the First Temple in Jerusalem was standing. According to Patai, there was an extended struggle lasting almost four hundred years concerning whether to include the Asherah figure inside the temple, where—according to the Torah—special women priestesses wove garments for Asherah. Male sacred prostitutes serving Asherah are also mentioned in the Torah. That era ended with the reforms of King Josiah around 600 B.C.E. (He was killed in 609 B.C.E.). Josiah sought the advice of the prophetess Huldah to interpret a scroll of the Law and accordingly removed the main Asherah from the temple and pulverized it. Eager to prevent the destruction and exile that Huldah and the other prophets had foretold, he made a sweep of the countryside and eliminated the rural shrines and statues with similar zeal. Huldah's cousin, the prophet Jeremiah, berated the Judeans of that time for worshipping the foreign deities on all the high hills and engaging in a wide range of magical practices. The criticism was not solely about issues of pagan practice but referenced a number of moral failures, including neglect of the poor and widows.

Meanwhile, the goddess Anat, Asherah's daughter, took up residence in the temple of the Egyptian Jews at the military colony of Elephantine, whose house of worship was dedicated to YHVH and Anat Beth-El. This community, which flourished from around 495 to 399 B.C.E. in the Aswan area, may have been started by Jews functioning as "mercenaries" working for the Egyptian government. There Anat, the fierce warrior deity, was honored. While the exiled Elephantine community was unique in taking the liberty of creating a mini–Jerusalem Temple (which was destroyed by their Egyptian neighbors) and providing more equality for women, it was not alone in venerating the goddess Asherah or her daughter. Other ancient sites have yielded cave inscriptions dedicated to YHVH v-Asherato (Yahweh and his consort Asherah).

From the prophetic perspective, these are deviations from the true path and ultimately lead to destruction and exile. From a historical perspective, there seems to be a conflict with acknowledging a relationship to the pagan past. Was the need to portray the neighbors as lewd and perverse a way of dealing with the loss of sexual freedom, and with loss of the initiatory rituals for men conducted by the holy women—*qadeishot*—who had now become the less-than-sacred prostitutes? In ancient times, Canaanite women, including married women, gave a week of the year to the goddess, in which they served at a temple or local shrine. One of their functions was to induct visiting men into the goddess's ways by sleeping with them. Is Orthodox Judaism's view that women are inherently more spiritual a remnant of this memory? Is the kabbalistic view of women providing men with entry to the Shekhinah also reminiscent of these ancient practices? Numerous Torah commentators project far more than a taste for group sex on the neighbors. Suggestions of bestiality and incest come up, and of course homosexuality. Is this process of recasting the pagan into *shikutz* (abomination) a strategy for keeping us from our longing for the goddess, who had accompanied us on our journey through the desert wilderness? And how did this biblical labeling ultimately enter the Yiddish vocabulary to discourage intermarriage with the alluring *shiksa* or *sheigetz*?

Even in the great Jewish temples, according to scholar Raphael Patai, there were times when the Divine Feminine was venerated as Asherah. In

43

*The Hebrew Goddess*, he makes the case for a three- to four-hundred-year period when the goddess was brought into the First Temple by various competing kings and then was removed by others. During those turbulent times, the large Asherah statues resided in the main sanctuary, attended by the priests and priestesses, including the mysterious women who "weave houses/garments for the Asherah." They are mentioned in II Kings 23:7, which chronicles the reforms of King Josiah, who terminated the Asherah worship in the Jerusalem Temple.

From the vantage point of the Hebrew prophets, the recurring preoccupation with Asherah, mother goddess of the Ugaritic pantheon—whose qualities often overlap with those of the younger Astarte, the goddess of Lebanon—is an indication of the people's disloyalty to the one God, their inability to commit. Such disloyalty shows itself repeatedly and is stronger among the northern tribes, where pagan leanings were more typical of the leaders. The Book of Kings cites the placement of the Asherim on the high hills under the rule of King Rehavam (noting that his mother was the Ammonite Naama) and tells the story of King Yarovam, who created golden calves and installed them at local shrines (I Kings 12:28–33). The prophets denounce these actions as evil departures from the true path. However, the Hebrew God is called by the name of Asherah's consort, the chief god, El (sometimes called Bull-El). And the biblical God's characteristics bear an uncanny similarity to those of the cloud-rider god Baal, who is Asherah's first and most famous son. Asherah and El sit at the top of the pantheon of paired gods and goddesses, in their case numbering seventy. Judaism would later convene the seventy elders. Jewish tradition speaks of the seventy languages of humankind, and on Sukkot seventy bulls were sacrificed to honor the nations of the world. Is it not possible that the adoption of the mystical seventy comes from the Ugaritic, or an older source that precedes them both?

The straight and narrow monotheistic path did not come easily in a land still sacrificing to the many *baalim* (gods) and still encountering their prophets. Remember the prophet Balaam, who gave Judaism the quintessential morning blessing "Ma tovu ohalecha yaakov, mishknotecha Yisrael" (How goodly are your tents, Jacob, your dwelling places, Israel) when called upon to curse the Israelite encampment? The Torah acknowledges the Ruach ha Kodesh in all beings, including foreign prophets, yet the commentaries vilify Balaam as a man who has a sexual relationship with his donkey. The ass is the heroine of Numbers chapters 22–24, where she is portrayed as seeing an angel and speaking to her owner to warn him against a no-win assignment. The Torah prohibits mediums, psychics, and necromancers even as the great kings of Israel consult with them, as in the case of King Saul, who consults with the medium of Endor. In another incident of that period, Saul's daughter Michal, who was King David's first wife, helps David escape her father's wrath by placing the teraphim and a goat-hair pillow in the bed in David's place when Saul comes to kill him. Is the presence of the idols in her house an indication that she was familiar with their use?

The dance with the pagan past went on even as the more specifically Judaic practices were developed. Did these attractions to paganism represent the lure of forbidden sex? Did they embody the longing for freedom of expression—which burst through with the incident of the golden calf—and perhaps escape from the rules of the tribal leader? Or was there something deeper, namely the longing for God the Mother? Were these deviations from the main path developed by marginal Jews in exile, or do they reflect various points and places in Jewish history when the path was more inclusive? These questions currently have no answers. Judaism continues to resist its pagan roots, even as Christianity forgets its Jewish origins. Perhaps there will be a future time in which memory is no longer a threat. Just as Judaism needs to acknowledge its pagan past, contemporary spiritual movements, to be true to themselves, need to be aware of the nature orientation in Judaism and recognize the history of the Shekhinah as part of the traditional Jewish path.

It is not only the ordinary person who carries this image of Judaism as aggressively patriarchal. Various feminist theologians have attributed the downfall of the goddess to the emergence of Judaism. While Judaism's evolution coincided with the end of the Great Mother's external reign in the Middle East, it is highly doubtful that Judaism was the main instrument of change. That process extended over thousands of years and endured numerous attacks from overtly hostile and warlike cultures from northern Europe.

For contemporary Jewish women, this struggle is still alive, albeit in different forms. There are, on one hand, the goddess-oriented women, many of whom reject formal Jewish religious affiliation and feel that they serve the Shekhinah through alternative spiritual practices. Alongside them on the spectrum are the practicing Jewish women who have brought the Shekhinah and female language back to Jewish liturgical life. Increasingly, these two viewpoints—and various other shadings—are meeting each other in gatherings celebrating Jewish and female identity to work through the seeming contradiction.

# *Meditation*
## The Sacred in Nature

It is the spring equinox, and you are going out into nature on this beautiful day to celebrate the change in seasons. The hills are blanketed with velvety rich green colors, a gift from the winter rains. All around you is the miracle of the earth coming back to life.

As you ascend a familiar trail, you are struck by the number of flowers that have opened only recently. Your eyes take in the luscious hues—pinks and lavenders, deep purples and dark reds. The smells of the reemerging growth are intoxicating, and the air is so pure that you feel yourself coming fully alive. In this precious moment, you realize that all the colors represent Shekhinah, embracing all the natural world.

# Canaan

You are also aware of the many small animals in this environment—bugs and spiders, lizards and rabbits. All around you is the sound of birds singing as they perch in the flowering shrubs and trees. Hawks circle in the sky, and occasional flocks of geese and migrating ducks make their way to the water nearby.

As you watch the movement around you, you realize that everything that lives or breathes is enlivened by the breath of Shekhinah. Nothing that exists is devoid of her presence.

There is such a sense of peace, such an inner knowing of the Song of Songs: "The rains are over and gone, and the time for nature's song has come."

You feel a deep gratitude to the Creator for the strength of your body and the freedom to be outdoors. From this place of happiness, the traditional prayer comes to you, praising God who lifts the downfallen, heals the sick, and liberates the captives:

*Somech noflim, rofeh cholim, u' mateer asurim.*

You intone your personal prayer for those who are in need, asking that  health, happiness, liberation, and prosperity come to all.

You continue on your way, meeting up later in the day with groups from many backgrounds and ethnic groups converging on the mountaintop for the equinox ceremony, in the hope that different belief systems can unite to enjoy and protect the earth and its fullness.

You walk together up a high hill. The sun sets in golden glory over the ocean to the west, and the moon rises in her brightness above the hills in the east. When you arrive at the site, a fire is already blazing, and the drummers have begun the essential beat for bringing the group together. A giant shofar is blown to herald the beginning of the ritual, and the sounds are picked up and echoed by numerous young people blowing *shofarot*.

The music and dance amplify the joyous energy of the assembled group, and the chanting creates the atmosphere for welcoming the Divine Presence. Different teachers come forward, sharing teachings of the Divine Mother from their respective traditions.

# Chapter 3

You are listening with your heart,

feeling the teachings with your mind,

understanding within your body organs, deep down,

that ALL IS ONE.

The images are different, the practices vary, but the origin is ONE.

All memories of the Great Mother in her many forms

with her thousands of faces are welcomed here:

pouring out her abundance,

giving blessings for creativity,

ensuring equity and justice,

providing compassion and healing,

and embracing with unending love

all the life forms that emerged from her womb.

And you know that you are one with her.

*For the Presence of the Lord filled the House of the Lord . . .*
*then Solomon declared:*
*The Lord has chosen to abide in a thick cloud*
*I have now built for you a stately house*
*A place where you may dwell forever.*

—I Kings

*Shekhinah in the temple hovered over them like a Mother hovering over her*
*children, and so all faces were lit up, and all found blessing both above and*
*here below.*

—Zohar

*He* [King Solomon] *made the palanquins of silver . . . the inside thereof being*
*inlaid with love.*

R. Azaiah said: "This refers to the Shekhinah."

—Song of Songs Rabah

*The high priest did not see the Divine Presence when he entered the sanctuary, but a cloud came down and when it lighted on the mercy seat the Cherubim beat their wings together and broke out into song.*

—Zohar

# Chapter 4

# *Temple*

## Divine Mother Comes Home

*P*rior to the building of Beit ha Mikdash (First Temple), the Israelites had not established a central location for a national religion with a subsidized priesthood. They were probably observing Shabbat and holidays at home and occasionally going on spiritual journeys to local sites. During this early period, before the monarchy, the Ark of the Covenant, so connected with Shekhinah's communication with Moses, was housed in various sites, including Shiloh, Gilgal, and Givon. Those sanctuaries were attended by priests and/or prophets who presided over the cultic sacrifices. The First Book of Samuel, noting Hannah's famous prayer (I Sam. 2:1–10), describes her family's journey to the regional holy site to pray and make offerings. The anointing of King Saul by the prophet Samuel—to whom God appears at Shiloh—and his later designation of King David affirms the importance of those regional holy places and the authority given to the prophet at that time, before the construction of the temple.

Believing that the Ark of the Covenant was where God manifested the Divine Presence on earth, the Israelites had carried the sacred ark and its accoutrements in the Mishkan with them into the Promised Land, but it is unlikely that most people could have had access to the cultic sanctuary more than a few times a year, unless they lived close to a regional shrine. As they developed their national culture, it became important to their rulers to establish a more permanent dwelling place for Shekhinah in the Promised Land. King David's profound faith in God and his popularity among the people were reinforced by moving the ark up to the City of David, where he danced ecstatically in what now is Jerusalem. While David yearned to build

Chapter 4

the permanent home for the Lord, that honor was denied him, according to rabbinical midrash, because of his involvement with war and violence. That emphasis on peace as essential to true spirituality (which would be further developed in the Talmud) is reinforced in the description of King Solomon's building of the temple in a time of both abundance and peace. The huge imperial project involved cooperation with Lebanon in the acquisition of the cedars and cypresses for the building. The Tanakh (Hebrew Scriptures) also mentions the training of laborers in Lebanon. There was explicit instruction in the Torah that no metal tools be used in the construction, so there would be a reverent atmosphere throughout. Numerous legends expand on the theme of miraculous engineering, including the use of a magical worm that could cut the gigantic rocks without tools!

The lavish building process undertaken during the reign of the wise King Solomon seems to have been an enlargement of the building and embellishment of the Mishkan, Shekhinah's sanctuary in the desert. In the earlier construction, God spelled out to Moses the exact colors and shapes of the decoration and the materials to be used. Legend has it that the Shekhinah, who is omnipresent in the world, would contract into the small space beneath the ark. That area, known as the Mercy Seat, became the sacred opening where Moses would receive communication from the Divine. The Mishkan was always protected by the two golden *keruvim* (cherubs) who spread their massive wings over the Ark of the Covenant, reinforcing the belief that the Divine Glory resided above the cherubs. These keruvim were redone by Solomon on a larger scale for the Jerusalem Temple. Their meaning and role as emissaries of the divine realm became the focus of esoteric literature for generations. Early on, the Rabbis argued about the nature of those keruvim, some considering them animal, others human. Some sages described them as childlike and both male, while others said one was male and one female. The essential teaching was that when Israel was in harmony with God, the cherubs would embrace like a man and woman in love; when Israel was out of alignment with God, they would separate.

# Temple

The arrangement of the ritual objects within the Mishkan area and the tent of meeting were essential to cultic practice and the calling in of Shekhinah's presence. The process of protecting the Ark of the Covenant and the portable sanctuary around it was greatly magnified with the building of the First Temple in Jerusalem. The description in I Kings, chapters 5–8, tells us that Solomon considers this God's house, and the Torah describes the luxurious materials culled from many lands to embellish the temple. All the wood is overlaid with gold, and all the lavers are brass. Decorations with traditional forms are also described. After the construction is complete, the ark, containing only the two stone tablets of the Law, is brought in by the priests and placed under the massive gold cherubim, their huge wingspan covering it. All the new pure-gold Mishkan implements surround the ark—the altar table, candlesticks, snuffers, spoons, basins, and so forth. At that point, a miraculous cloud descends, reminiscent of Shekhinah's clouds of glory in the desert, and even the officiating priests are overwhelmed and must go out. Choirs of Levites singing and playing and a cadre of priests attending to the offerings from the people, with the most luxurious appointments of fabric and design, accompany this installation of the Shekhinah in her permanent home.

In the Jerusalem Temple, according to the sages, the Shekhinah was announced with the tinkling of bells, which alternated with golden pomegranates on the hem of the high priest's garment. The legend was that Shekhinah could be "heard" in the fluttering sounds that accompanied the high priest, referring to the winged presence of Shekhinah, and "smelled" in the special incense that was offered. And she could be "seen" in the smoke that ascended from the *olah* sacrifice, or holocaust offering. The Temple Mount was Shekhinah's home territory; the temple itself her dwelling place; the Holy of Holies the intimate chamber where she encountered her consort, YHVH. The Holy Blessed One himself is said to have descended to install her in this elegant and well-appointed abode, a house "lined with love" that emanated from her presence.

These large temple gatherings, probably designed to replicate the devotion experienced at Sinai, became the ceremonial pathway for attracting Shekhinah's presence. She was like cosmic glue, holding the planet together. Being in the home of the Divine Presence provided a sense of unity to the disparate clans and tribes, especially at holidays, when they joined together in national religious practice. If we can imagine the many thousands of agrarian people who made their pilgrimage to the temple for the three great celebrations (the Shelosh Regalim of Pesach, Shavuot, and Sukkot), we can begin to understand the profound implications of these huge conclaves. Coming from all over the country, many on foot, the pilgrims (estimated at hundreds of thousands) had the opportunity to recommit themselves to the spiritual practices and their sense of connection with each other. They experienced the worship in a large and moving celebration, officiated by well-trained priests and Levites.

The power of the temple and the cultic practice remained as the central symbol for thousands of years after the temple's destruction. Of course, the memory was romanticized by loss. The Jewish imagination, reinforced by the poetry of the prayer book that replaced the temple practice, emerged from the yearnings of an exiled people. Away from home, they pined for and embellished the golden era of an ancient past filled with the glory of the great temple.

This was especially true for the First Temple, traditionally thought to have been built c. 950 B.C.E. and destroyed by the Babylonians under King Nebuchadnezzar in 586 B.C.E. The Second Temple period (539 B.C.E.–70 C.E.), which followed the Babylonian exile, was dominated by rival spiritual and political philosophies, while repeated invasions by neighboring kingdoms and larger regional powers always threatened the security of the small Jewish state. The Second Temple was reconstructed by Herod the Great on a massive scale around the turn of the first century C.E., but the commentaries suggest that it did not have the same level of holiness as its predecessor, and that the presence of Shekhinah was less powerful than it had been. The destruction of the Second Temple by the Romans in 70 C.E. terminated the official reign of Shekhinah in Jerusalem.

The Hebrew prophets wrote vividly of the events that preceded the destruction and exile from the land. We read these passages thoughtfully on Yom Kippur and in weekly Haftorah readings as a reminder to stay on the path. In a paradoxical presentation, the sages taught, on one hand, that Shekhinah handed over the First Temple to the Babylonians. On the other hand, she will punish all the aggressors in times to come. The rabbinic and prophetic writings presented this temple drama as the wayward journey of a people being called to wholeness and morality by the Shekhinah, their guardian spirit, their eagle of protection, their nurturing mother. In early rabbinic literature, Shekhinah calls repeatedly to the Israelites to return and repent. But they are too busy or distracted to change their ways, so she has no recourse but to allow the negative elements to play their role in the karmic drama. The Babylonians, drunk on conquest in the region, bombard the walls, enter the Temple Mount, and set the area on fire. They remove the gold and silver precious vessels, some of which they will convert from sacred service of the Divine to containers for King Nebuchadnezzar's sumptuous feasts. While the Rabbis tell us that Shekhinah will punish all the aggressive empires in time to come, they also focus on the issue of collective destiny. According to Jewish legends, Shekhinah stands at the door of the temple and allows the invaders to enter and destroy because her house has already been undermined by lack of faith, internal power struggles, and inattention to the suffering of the poor. She is giving them the shell; the interior has already been gutted. Her fire, normally the fire of warmth and protection, like the amud ha esh in the desert, has become the consuming fire of destruction, experienced through the hands of the enemy.

For the next two thousand years, Jewish mystics experienced visions of the Shekhinah at the wall of the temple, clad in black and weeping for her residence, for her children, for her people in exile, just as the prophet Jeremiah had foretold. The mystics incorporated this lament into the

warmth + protection- asks the same

midnight prayers, tikkun chatzot, calling upon the matriarchs Rachel and Leah for help. The Mother, source of our connectedness, had been sent into exile, separated from her consort, YHVH. However, the collective psyche also needs to retain the idealized holidays, or it will be overcome with the metaphor of repeated destruction and loss, persecution and suffering. There is a need to remember when all joined together to sing and pray. Maybe this deep recall is what motivates even disconnected Jews to come back to synagogues for the High Holidays or to hold Passover Seders in their homes. The collective Jewish imagination still stores a glorious temple and a halcyon time when everything was suffused by the golden light of Jerusalem. From the Talmud to the Zohar, the Jewish sages taught that even though the Matrona (another name for Shekhinah) might go underground or be in exile from her consort, she always accompanies her people in their wanderings and is available to them on Shabbat, holidays, the New Moon, and all sacred occasions that recall the glorious temple.

# Meditation

## Entering the Ancient/Future Temple

Imagine yourself a pilgrim in the Israel of your dreams, ancient or future. You have traveled a long way to Jerusalem. As you approach the Temple Mount, you are enveloped by a special energy that uplifts and supports you. Entering the city, you are welcomed to a lovely inn, where you sleep off the weariness of the journey and receive wholesome food and drink. Early in the morning, you are invited to immerse yourself in a luxurious ritual bath. You emerge from this mikveh feeling reborn, and you don flowing robes that make you feel as if you are floating on gossamer wings. Now you are ready to approach the Holy Temple from the south. There is a miraculous rainbow overhead; the sun is shining, and the weather is clear and warm. A light breeze floats across the valley, carrying the scent of pomegranates from Jericho in the south.

As you come up to the Huldah gates, you are conscious of the other visitors, all on a sacred journey. You feel the good will all around you, as well as the blessings of many enlightened teachers. You hear choirs singing psalms of praise to the accompaniment of many instruments. You enter the temple on the right and move through the marble courts. You can feel the warmth of the Great Mother in every stone. You inhale the scent of the most intoxicating incense and hear the subtle sound of tinkling bells, indications that the Shekhinah is making her presence felt. As you approach the great courtyard where the priests and priestesses are receiving the offerings, you can sense how each person's worry or concern is lifted from them as they present their gift to the facilitator. You cry and laugh with them as if they were telling your story.

In this ancient-future temple, only grains and flowers and fruits are "sacrificed," because everyone has evolved past using animals as this expression of devotion. It is almost your turn to bring your offering forward to the holy altar. You thought carefully on the way about what you will give over to God. What do you no longer need to carry? What do you need to make amends for? This is your opportunity to be healed, but you are no longer thinking; you are only be-ing in the divine energy. The priestly healer, the emissary of the Shekhinah, awaits you. Tell her or him what is in your heart.

*Shekhinah . . . at the destruction of the Temple revisited all the spots where she had dwelt formerly and wept for her habitation and for Israel who had gone into exile.*

—Zohar

*Shekhinah never leaves them. It was with them in Babylon, and returned with them from the captivity; and for the sake of those righteous who were left in the land, it abode in the land, as it never left them.*

—Zohar

*A judge who delivers a true judgement causes the Shekhinah to dwell in Is-rael* [among the people] *and he who does not deliver judgements in perfect truth causes the Shekhinah to depart.*

—Talmud

*Wherever Torah is studied earnestly, the Shekhinah comes and joins, and all the more so on the road.*

—Zohar

# Chapter 5

# *Babylonian Exile*

## The Ethical Mother

*T*he two central experiences in the formation of the collective Jewish psyche are the revelation at Sinai, regarded as a group epiphany, and the destruction of the First Temple in 586 B.C.E., which we might consider a holocaust or loss of world. The "high" of shared collective experience of the Divine was repeated and reinforced in the drama and power of Jerusalem Temple worship. The development of the Babylonian synagogues and the Siddur, or prayer book, represented the rabbinical attempt to reconstitute that sense of exalted worship experience. To replace an elegant priesthood with its dramatic fire rituals and the beautiful Levitical choral and instrumental music was an impressive challenge. The glory of the temple was still in the memory of the elders, and it was conveyed at least to the first generation of exiles. That loss was embedded in the daily prayer book (in which we call every day for the rebuilding of the temple and reinstatement of the cultic practice). Those sentiments, retained without the same quality of personal tragedy, were institutionalized in the annual fast day of Tisha B 'Av (Ninth of Av), commemorating the loss of the First and Second Temples on that date. Marked by fasting and prayer for the central loss in Jewish life, the serious summer observance carries with it mourning for all the losses and suffering that came with the dispersion of the tribes of Israel around the world.

That destruction, like a childhood memory of trauma, was probably the most deeply imprinted in the collective Jewish consciousness, coming in the early history of the nation before the many other exiles, and following the great Hebrew prophets' warnings of disaster. The people of Israel were deprived of their freedom, their homes, their land, their monarchy, and their holy temple. The Ark of the Covenant had disappeared or been hidden, never to be found. Some legends allude to the prophet Jeremiah hiding the ark before the conquest. Other stories suggest that the doors of the temple sank into the ground. Other chronicles, however, describe King Nebuchadnezzar's forces removing the ritual objects from the Mishkan and transporting them to Babylon for the king's use. Destruction of the land was total, wiping out not only the physical and economic life of the people, but every value they held dear and every hope they had for the future. A significant percentage of the leaders and teachers were force-marched to Babylon; the first group deported is estimated by historians at ten thousand. On that journey, they began the lament that would echo for thousands of years—the longing for Zion: "By the waters of Babylon we lay down and wept for thee, Zion" (Psalm 137). Could they sing their sacred songs in a strange land?

The break from the land also initiated the questioning that echoed through Jewish sacred literature about the location of the Shekhinah. For hundreds of years, the sages asked if the Shekhinah could dwell outside the homeland, and specifically away from the Jerusalem Temple. The exiles too asked if they would be able to feel the Divine Presence away from home. They must have wondered if they would ever feel protected and safe again. Would they ever become whole after this shattering of all the institutions that held their lives together? Like a young child being separated violently from its mother and its home, the young nation must have felt cut off from its source of nourishment. Those left behind endured starvation and poverty in an Israel whose infrastructure had been obliterated. While the majority left in Judea were poor and uneducated, some of their leaders chose to remain with them. The hardships for the common people were profound and enduring. The prophetic writings tell of widespread famine and horrific social conditions, a time of awful suffering.

Because most of the deportees were educated and skilled, they were eventually able to rebuild their economic and religious lives. Throughout the seventy-year Diaspora, the Jewish exiles were blessed with the presence of powerful prophetic personalities—including the prophet Ezekiel, who emerged at this time—sustaining their belief in divine providence and in their eventual return to the land of Israel. The Babylonian monarchy provided special status for the young prophet Daniel, who was supposedly captured as a teenager and brought to the court to interpret the King Nebuchadnezzar's dreams. Daniel's personal story is similar to the narrative in Genesis concerning Joseph and the role he played as dream interpreter for the Egyptian pharaoh. Most of us are familiar with Daniel's interpretation of "the handwriting on the wall" at Balshazzar's feast (Dan. 5:25–29), which predicted the downfall of Babylon. Since Judaic tradition taught that prophesy was a function of Ruach ha Kodesh—the Holy Spirit—emanating from Shekhinah to inspire the individual, the community was encouraged to believe that God was with them, and that divine guidance was being expressed through the prophets in their midst. They were able to maintain their religious practice, at least in the first generation, and to nourish sages who engaged in significant spiritual inquiry, which led to the development of the Babylonian Talmud.

These exiled scholars continued the dialogue about the location of the Shekhinah. Some argued that the Divine Presence, the "bed of God," could live only in the land of Israel, and in fact could be felt only in the vicinity of the Holy Temple in Jerusalem. Others argued that the Shekhinah, as God's presence, was omnipresent, in every place in the world simultaneously. Surely their Eagle of Protection would accompany the Jewish people in their exile. Stories circulated of individuals who heard the fluttering of wings or the sound of bells over particular sites. Many believed that the presence who provided divine protection would continue to hover over them and guide their way, just as the clouds of glory had done in the Sinai wilderness. Zarkah, the one who throws the light, would bring the light to the oppressed wherever they wandered. And Shekhinah's role as punisher guaranteed that the evildoers would ultimately be judged. With the evolution of the Babylonian exile and its strong emphasis on Jewish communal life came the later designation of Shekhinah as Knesset Yisrael, or Community of Israel. Guardianship of community life, also in the hands of the religious teachers, required more stringent adherence to high standards of personal behavior. Ethical precepts for living were now tied to the Shekhinah.

Later, as the Talmud developed, these ideas became more specific, with the dictum that Shekhinah is present whenever a minyan (quorum) of ten men gathers to pray or comes together in the *beit midrash*, or study hall. From a people who had been visitors in a strange land came the teaching that those who extended hospitality to strangers would receive the countenance of the Shekhinah. From those who had experienced poverty came the instruction that one who gives charity to a beggar—even one small coin— would surely experience the Divine Presence. From those who needed reassurance in times of illness and death came the reminder that Ruach ha Kodesh sits at all sickbeds, waiting with open arms for those who cross over. From a people who had been the victims of imperial assault came the Talmudic teaching that violence, pollution, and incest alienate Shekhinah, and that abhorrent human behavior would force Shekhinah to fly off to the seven heavens where the angels bask in ziv ha Shekhinah, the radiant light of the Divine Glory.

As the commentaries expanded and religious life became more intellectual, the concept of Shekhinah as divine immanence, or God within and around the self, developed within an increasingly subtle ethical framework. In this schematic, people could attract Shekhinah by their mitzvot (good deeds) or distance the Divine Presence when they violated the Law. The ability to attract Shekhinah to the earth was based, according to the Talmud, on following the Torah and leading lives of study, worship, charity, and hospitality. Lest people become carried away with pride in their actions, the sages reminded them that the Divine Presence could not live with arrogance; an inflated self left no place for the Glory to enter. Only the humble merited the Indwelling One. For this reason, the sages surmised, the Shekhinah appeared in the lowly thorn bush to Moses, the most humble of God's servants. For this reason, Shekhinah is represented on the Passover table by matzah, simple bread also known as *lechem oni*, or poor bread. While some commentators linked Shekhinah to the gift of personal charisma and tried to connect that quality to males who were tall and of noble bearing, the primary relationship was to simplicity and humility.

From the Talmud came the hundred years of rabbinical commentary on the immanence of God, presented usually in gender-neutral fashion, mainly through the metaphor of light. While the term *Shekhinah* was feminine, the Talmud did not define God's more accessible presence as female, as did later kabbalistic literature. Interestingly, however, the sages began to portray Shekhinah almost as a separate presence from the male deity, especially in those midrashim in which Shekhinah rises to defend the children of Israel. In various parables, the Divine Presence would appear before the throne of glory to defend someone. Stories of the Shekhinah's defense of King Solomon are part of the evolving presentation of a nearly separate attribute. The issue of whether Shekhinah could be depicted as a quasi-divine power carried over into the discussion of the feminine aspect of God well into the twentieth century.

At the same time, if we look over the great body of Midrash, we find that many of the characteristics that were attributed to Shekhinah are similar to the traits of the ancient Middle Eastern goddesses. She is the great winged being who protects her children, the guardian of the crops who calls for equitable sharing of resources, the punisher of sins who descends to earth on numerous occasions to carry out disciplinary expeditions. Ironically, it was the writing of male scholars that kept the Great Mother alive, though well hidden within Jewish literature. Was it really the male rabbinic imagination that nurtured these concepts of Shekhinah, or did the sages give written form to what was remembered, experienced, and understood by the larger folk culture, which included women's wisdom? We know that in the early stages of the development of the Talmud, scholarly work was probably still done in areas close to the home. Reconstructed Talmudic-era villages in northern Israel portray a simple existence where family life, eating, working, studying, and praying all took place in close proximity to one another. The early years in Babylon—prior to the development of the great academies at Sura and Pumpedita —might still have reflected that kind of village organization. While men were clearly in charge of prayer, study, and writing, their activities may have been conducted in open forums near women and children; and the recall and writing of the Oral Law (associated with Shekhinah) could have drawn on collective memory and folklore, perhaps even including stories told by elders and women. Talmudic anecdotes about the life of Ima Shalom, who lived in the turbulent first century, suggest her interactions with the writers. As the daughter of a great sage and the wife of one of the most prominent teachers of that era, she was highly educated and may have participated in scholarly conversations. The Talmud also quotes the teachings and legal opinions of Beruriah, a famous second-century scholar with outstanding family history and credentials, who taught the Law in the academy of her husband, Rabbi Meir. Both women would later be regarded by those focused on demeaning the role of women as *yotseit min ha klal*, exceptional or out of the ordinary—in colloquial terms, the exception that proves the rule.

While we will never know exactly how influential women were in shaping the Talmud, we do know that redactions of the oral tradition included many stories and interpretations that we can use to reconstruct a picture of Shekhinah moving through Jewish history.

Related to the ending of the first Babylonian exile is the legend of Purim told in the Book of Esther. Pious, chaste, and noble, Esther represents the Shekhinah. She hides her identity like the new moon, waiting to emerge from the dark and become the defender and protector of her people. Similarly, we are taught that the face of Shekhinah is often hidden from humanity as she maintains the life of the universe. According to Jewish legends, Queen Esther wraps herself in the mantle of Shekhinah—when she dons royal clothing, she is really assuming the garb of Malkhut—and reaches out through her prayers and fasting to draw down the miracle of salvation from the highest level. As Queen Esther's role develops, she, like the full moon of Purim, becomes more self-confident and grows into her power. At first a guest in the king's castle, ultimately she inherits it along with the kingdom. Rather than waiting for the decision of the Rabbis, Esther declares the holiday of Purim to commemorate the people's triumph. Later in the Zohar, Queen Esther's standing before the king to plead for her people is interpreted in the context of Shekhinah standing before God at the throne of glory, speaking on behalf of the people of Israel.

Forty thousand members of the exiled Babylonian Jewish community returned to the Holy Land to live and rebuild the temple, while many others stayed in Persia to continue enjoying the good life in affluent Babylon rather than return to an impoverished Israel. Even among those who returned, many had intermarried, and that became the focus of criticism by the prophets Ezra and Nehemiah. Under the leadership of these fiery leaders, the Jewish people were encouraged to strengthen their religious life and rebuild a country now deeply scarred by poverty and lack of education. Directed by sages and prophets, they were called upon to use their education and skills on behalf of their compatriots and to seek insights for a battered nation through their study of the holy books.

# Meditation
## Finding the Inner Sage

Picture yourself in a beautiful study full of precious sacred texts from various spiritual paths. Among these books there is a particular subject you have always wanted to study, but you have wondered if you could absorb it without the help of a seasoned teacher.

## Chapter 5

Because of your strong intention to study, some very special gates of understanding are being opened for you by the heavenly powers. As you approach the shelves to select a book, you are surrounded by the energies of the scholars and saints who authored many of these tomes. These great souls, now in other dimensions, occasionally visit this planet to bestow their light and blessings on those who pursue knowledge for the highest good. When this happens, the human student experiences an expanded awareness and deeper insights into the writings than they have ever known before.

You may wish to call upon the beings from the spiritual tradition that you resonate with. Since most writings were set down by men, you might make a special request for women teachers to be present. If you are of Jewish background, you could invoke the female teachers of Talmud, including Beruriah and Ima Shalom.

Embraced by the love of the sages, you choose your book and find a niche looking out onto a garden. You settle into a comfortable chair that feels as if it were designed for your body.

As you open this wisdom text, you are moved by the tenderness of the study guides. Like guardian angels, they are emissaries of the Shekhinah come to ease your learning. As they escort you into the Divine Presence, even the most complex concepts become light and simple.

You intone a prayer of gratitude for this time of study and the blessing of the guides who enlighten you through the music of the mind. You begin to read and notice how much you understand and how profound your thoughts are. All the synapses in your brain have become illuminated.

Enjoy your thoughts as you study, and write them down when you complete your process.

As you conclude, you see how the sages of all traditions open the gates of wisdom and understanding for men and women. Know that all beings are children of the Shekhinah, and that this gift is available to people of all backgrounds and faiths.

*According to his will, God makes his voice heard to his Glory/Shekhinah which blesses God and presents itself in any image necessary. And the spectacle of the Glory is like consuming fire and it is called the Shekhinah.*

—Rabbi El'azar ben Yehudah of Worms

*Prayer is God's partner, and She sits on his left side like a bride, and He is her bridegroom. And she is called the Daughter of the King and sometimes she is called "Bat Kol" after her mission, for the name of the Shekhinah that is with Him.*

—Rabbi El'azar ben Yehudah of Worms

*It is a form nobler even than* [that of] *the angels, magnificent in character, resplendent with light, which is called the Glory of the Lord . . . and that the sages characterized as Shekhinah.*

—Saadia Gaon

## Chapter 6

# The Medieval Years

## Divine Light and Prayer

Over centuries of dispersion—whether east or west—the concept or memory of Shekhinah was sustained. While we cannot assess how this was embedded in daily life, we can discern from the sacred literature that the concept remained very much alive for scholars, who probably reflected popular belief in some way. Most Jewish historians credit the Mizrachi sages of the Eastern countries with preserving the esoteric teachings that had been handed down from teacher to student for generations. During the early medieval period, that knowledge appeared in textual form in the *Sefer Bahir* and *Sefer Yetzirah* (Book of Creation). There was also some study and revival of the early chariot mysticism of the first and second centuries. Known as the Heichal or Merkavah literature, it described the journey of the early sages into the higher realms, reaching for the chariot vision of the prophet Ezekiel. Modern scholars have identified mystical brotherhoods functioning in Europe starting in the twelfth century and including the German Pietists, who may have recreated some of the practices of those earlier mystics.

In early medieval Jewish literature, even before the emergence of these pre-kabbalistic groups, the discussion of Shekhinah can be traced to the philosophical works of the great teachers of that era. Saadia Gaon (882–942 c.e.), the brilliant sage and spiritual leader of the Babylonian Jews, presented the concept of the *kavod nivra* (revealed glory) as his way of explaining the role of the Divine Presence. Saadia states—in language considered his innovation, and not Talmudic tradition—that the kavod is a created object, similar to the angels (*The Book of Beliefs and Opinions*, 121). The head of the seminary wrote in elegant Arabic to reach his affluent and philosophically sophisticated followers, aiming to convince them that faith and logic could be reconciled in Judaism. Maimonides—Rabbi Moshe Ben Maimon, known by the acronym *Rambam*, the great commentator whose works are still studied for their deep insight and wisdom—also wrote about Shekhinah as God's glory, or kavod. A physician by training, he wrote many books on Jewish law and practice and was honored by the eleventh-century Egyptian and Moroccan Jewish communities. In his *Guide for the Perplexed*, Rambam held that the Shekhinah "is a form superior to the angels, mighty in its creation, radiant with majesty and light." Seeing Shekhinah as the first of God's works, he wrote of "the created light which God caused to dwell in a given place in order to show the distinction of that place." While it is probable that Rambam had access to Saadia's writings, it may be that they were each responding to the zeitgeist in a manner that fit thinking in the Arabic intellectual world of which they were a part. Neither Saadia Gaon nor Rambam would be considered mystics, yet their thinking laid the groundwork for the evolution of Jewish mysticism.

The most profound writings on Jewish mystical thought and definitions of the Divine Glory emerged from the writings of Rabbi El'azar ben Yehudah of Worms. He and his teacher, Yehudah Ha Chasid (Judah the Pious), were the acknowledged leaders of the Chasidei Ashkenaz (Franco-German Jewish Pietists), a devotional community in Franco-Germany with highly developed ascetic values and practices. Their followers were located in the old Jewish settlement towns of Mainz, Speyer, and Worms, known for their great institutions of Jewish learning. Both teachers were descendants of the famous Kalonymous family, which was reputed to have brought the mystical teachings to Europe from the East. Rabbi El'azar is considered the foremost student of Yehudah Ha Chasid and the greatest teacher of his era. The author of numerous written works, he is well known for his legal rulings and interpretations of Jewish law, Halakhah, that came down to later generations as the *Sefer Rokeach*. Less known (and still not translated) are his books of philosophy and commentaries on mystical texts, including the *Sefer Yetzirah* (The Book of Creation). He was an enlightened being of the most extraordinary range, seemingly able to traverse many worlds, both scholarly and mystical. In addition to his literary and spiritual pursuits, he provided religious and temporal leadership to the Worms community along with his saintly wife, Rabbanit Dulstah of Worms, with whom he fathered three children. Dulstah was a direct descendant of Rashi, Rabbi Shlomo Yitzchaki of Troyes, the foremost exegete of the eleventh century, whose commentaries are still studied weekly by Jews around the world.

Rabbi El'azar's esoteric writings demonstrate great spiritual depth and intimate knowledge of the angelic realm and the Throne World embodied in the chariot vision of the prophet Ezekiel and emulated by the early Merkavah mystics. While some of this understanding might have come from El'azar's studies of earlier literature, or initiation through his family, it seems very likely that he experienced trance states in which these images and visions came to him. He is also reputed to have had magical transportation, known as *kevistat ha derech*, by which he traveled on a cloud to attend celebrations far from home, but this is folklore; he does not refer to it in his own writings. Although little has been written about techniques for achieving unique powers, El'azar's writings contain allusions to information conveyed to spiritual adepts across water (perhaps implying known medieval techniques of seeking guidance in water). He also connected specific conceptualizations of how prayer ascends and operates in the higher realms to devotional daily prayer practices, with meticulous attention to the significance of the format of the Hebrew prayers.

From Rabbi El'azar and his contemporaries, we have the vision of Shekhinah surrounded by angels and carrying messages aloft to the throne of glory, where it would be received by the Holy Blessed One. These sages also continued the development of the concept of Shekhinah as kavod (glory). Consistent with his community's focus, Rabbi El'azar provides us with the concept of Shekhinah as prayer itself, or as the conduit of prayer to the throne of glory. In elaborate and highly symbolic language, he hints at the erotic relationship within the Godhead, in which unification takes place of the God names and energies. We ourselves may participate in this divine process by virtue of our prayers and mitzvot (good deeds). That esoteric drama, which would reach its climax in the Zohar and ensuing teachings of the French and Spanish Kabbalists, was already anticipated in the *Sefer Bahir*, which was redacted in the year 1176 in Provence. Some of El'azar's books, including *Sefer Raziel* (The Book of Raziel the Angel), indicate his knowledge of the *Sefer Yetzirah*. It is very likely that he was also familiar with the *Bahir*, which contained many of the elements that later emerged in the Zohar regarding the ten Sephirot and the role of the Shekhinah.

The generations of scholars that followed Saadia Gaon, Rambam, and Rabbi El'azar of Worms continued the discussion of Shekhinah's qualities. Nachmanides, the outstanding thirteenth-century Spanish Talmudist and exegete (Rabbi Moses ben Naaman of Girona, known as Nachmanides or Ramban, 1194–1270), believed that Rambam's concept of Shekhinah as the created light generated more theological problems than it solved. Since there were many prayers in which we bless the kavod, he believed Saadia's and Rambam's views put Jewish practitioners in the position of praying to the created light rather than to God directly. Another contemporary of Nachmanides, Rabbi Moses ben R. Hasdai, scrutinized the language of the Midrash on Proverbs (in which the Shekhinah would stand up and speak to the Lord in defense of the Jewish people or specific individuals) and insisted that the dialogic formula was only a verbal convention, not meant to imply that Shekhinah was a created form. He understood the Shekhinah and the heavenly voice, *bat kol,* as one, both representing the Holy Spirit or Ruach ha Kodesh. God, being the Omnipresent One, could appear as Shekhinah, Holy Spirit, or celestial light whenever or wherever God wished.

What appears to be both consistent and repetitive are the many renditions of the belief that Shekhinah is the light of God or is experienced as light and splendor. Perhaps this was what they were feeling in their prayers and meditations. The emphasis by the scholars of the medieval period on the brightness of the Shekhinah—a view that had been widely held for a long time—may have been their specific historical way of connecting with the genderless Divine, or their way of making the Divine Presence more ethereal and white, less earthy, not of any specific colors or forms. Perhaps the very nature of early medieval life, with all its suffering, led both Jews and Christians to reach upward for the light. The architecture of medieval synagogues is similar to Christian cathedrals in that regard. The prevailing historical mindset may have made it more feasible for Jewish scholars to think of the Shekhinah as living in the heavens, surrounded by the angels and radiating light earthward. They also drew on the view of Shekhinah from the early Merkavah literature. In those mystical tracts, Shekhinah's light overwhelms the angels, who flap their wings to shield their eyes from her brightness. This concept is also found in earlier commentaries, which abound with examples of the Shekhinah's brilliance. For example, the elders of Israel experience the sapphire path in front of God in a great brightness like the heavens. Moses glows with light after his contact with Shekhinah on Mount Sinai, and Isaac beholds the glory when he is about to be sacrificed. While Shekhinah always had the option of living in the seven heavens, earlier generations emphasized the Shekhinah's willingness to be present on this planet if the people created the sacred space in which to receive her appropriately. This idea originated in Exodus, where God says, "If they build a sanctuary for me I will dwell among them" (Exod. 25:8). The medieval speculation about God's presence is not about gender, but about the issues of nearness and distance of God, usually referred to as immanence and transcendence.

Medieval scholarship was beautiful, elaborate, and thoughtful in its consideration of the Divine Presence. Like its Talmudic predecessors, what it lacked was the female voice and the participation of women. The closest we might come to speculating about this is in regard to the sacred marriage of Rabbi El'azar and Rabbanit Dulstah (or Dulcie), which is reflected in the poem he dedicated to her in 1213. Rabbi El'azar's poem was written some time after Rabbanit Dulstah was murdered by crusaders who attacked their home in 1196, while the rabbi was in another part of the house with a tutor and male students. The intruders quartered her when she attempted to save her children. Her two daughters were killed, and her son was wounded and eventually died. Bereft of his devoted partner, Rabbi El'azar expresses his grief in the poem, describing her work, her devotional practices, and her charitable activities. It is a variation on the Eyshet Chayil (Woman of Valor) prayer, drawn from Proverbs 31:10–31, that a man recites to his wife on Friday night as part of receiving the Sabbath. Rabbi El'azar's ode to his wife's good qualities gives us a picture of the life of a saintly Jewish woman of that era, who, in her many roles, embodied the Shekhinah on earth. She was devoted mother, wife, teacher, business woman, and community leader who sewed Torah scrolls, led brides to the *chuppah* (wedding canopy), and led women in prayer. She also supported her husband financially and provided food for his students. Her martyr's death was considered the highest sacrifice one could make on behalf of one's faith. The tragic death of the Shekhinah's messenger to her age may have led Rabbi El'azar deeper into study of the mystical texts, and his profound personal loss of family may be related to his interpretation of Shekhinah as the receiver of prayers.

Although we are blessed with this picture of Rabbanit Dulcie's short but luminous life, we are left with many unanswered questions about the way in which women called upon the Shekhinah. No doubt women found their channels to the Divine Presence by assisting at childbirth, baby namings, weddings, and deaths. We also know that medieval women, including Dulcie, prayed at the graves of their ancestors, especially on New Moon, and measured the wicks for candles used in the synagogue on those graves. Certainly, for medieval women, service to the synagogue was an important part of their devotional lives, in addition to the traditional female obligations.

To restate the philosophy of the Franco-German Pietists on this concept of the Shekhinah as Divine Glory, we might say that their great teachers recognized multiple visions of the Creator in the writings of the ancient prophets and early mystics. To them, it was important to acknowledge how this process worked, so that their prayers could be properly enunciated and directed. Their focus was on emphasizing the unity of the formless Creator and the Creator's paradoxical capacity to be in many places and take many forms to convey the Holy Spirit to deserving humans. While they were intent on clarifying the concurrent transcendent and immanent natures of God, they were also attempting to distinguish between inspired vision and images conjured up by magical techniques, which they considered delusional.

Perhaps some of this preoccupation was a function of what was happening around them. In Christian circles many great visionaries, including a number of holy women, were experiencing ecstatic visions of their Savior. One wonders why the Jewish writers were so focused on the visionary state, unless they too were experiencing visions of God in which the formless One appeared in some recognizable form. In their thinking, Shekhinah might appear as angelic or human, male or female, as a kind of astral archetype that conveyed messages from another realm. At the academic level, Jewish scholars were always concerned with presenting a unified theory of the Divine One, partly to distinguish their views from the Christian concept of the Trinity, and partly to assist them in their disputations with Christians about which was the "right religion." The great debate about the Divine Glory went on well into the later Middle Ages and was picked up by the preeminent thinkers of Italy, France, and Spain, who participated in the evolution of Jewish mystical thinking and the further conceptualization of Shekhinah.

# *Meditation*
## Entering the Light

Picture yourself as a young Jewish teenager in medieval western Europe, living in a climate that is cool at least half the year and, in the damp winter months, dark much of the time.

Like all the other buildings in your town, the house you live in is made of stone. The houses have very small windows, which keep the rain and snow out but also limit the light coming in. Your family has a central fire in the cooking area, which is also the dining and living area, and sometimes all of you sleep there for warmth. Your home is blessed by the piety of your parents, who have always taught you to seek God within and to respect all people.

Outside, the street is dirty and noisy. Local ruffians are often a challenge, even though you have known them from childhood. It is hard for you to understand why they hate Jews. When you are disturbed by outside events, your mother encourages you to find sanctuary in the house and in yourself. She makes special candles for the synagogue, measuring the wicks on the graves of saints, and gives you one to light.

You go into your alcove to light this special candle. You fix your sight on it . . . watching the black base, the blue aureole, and the golden flame. After a while, you experience yourself entering the light. You feel your heart melting, and you forget any problems you may have had. You are being held in Shekhinah's arms and protected by her wings. You become lighter and lighter, almost as if you could fly!

Now, you let the light of Shekhinah transport you to an inner palace of warmth and love, light and peace.

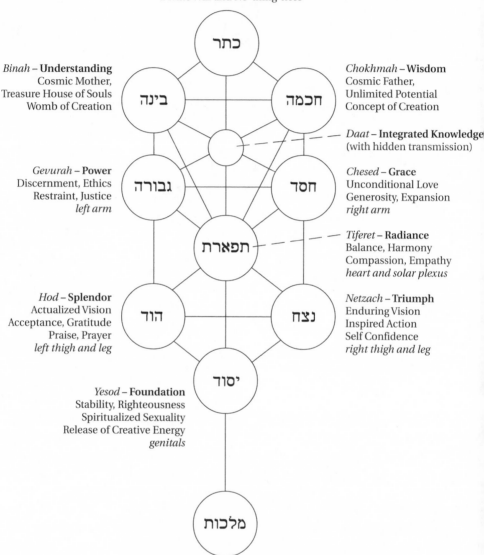

*Keter* – **Crown**
Soul's connection with Endless Light
Divine Will and No-thing-ness

כתר

*Binah* – **Understanding**
Cosmic Mother,
Treasure House of Souls
Womb of Creation

בינה

*Chokhmah* – **Wisdom**
Cosmic Father,
Unlimited Potential
Concept of Creation

חכמה

*Daat* – **Integrated Knowledge**
(with hidden transmission)

*Gevurah* – **Power**
Discernment, Ethics
Restraint, Justice
*left arm*

גבורה

*Chesed* – **Grace**
Unconditional Love
Generosity, Expansion
*right arm*

חסד

תפארת

*Tiferet* – **Radiance**
Balance, Harmony
Compassion, Empathy
*heart and solar plexus*

*Hod* – **Splendor**
Actualized Vision
Acceptance, Gratitude
Praise, Prayer
*left thigh and leg*

הוד

*Netzach* – **Triumph**
Enduring Vision
Inspired Action
Self Confidence
*right thigh and leg*

נצח

יסוד

*Yesod* – **Foundation**
Stability, Righteousness
Spiritualized Sexuality
Release of Creative Energy
*genitals*

מלכות

*Malkhut* – *Shekhinah* – **Earth** – **Nature**
Physical Manifestation of All Life Forms
Indwelling Presence, Lower Crown
Mother of Lower World
*feet*

# Chapter 7

# *Kabbalah*

## The Feminine on the Tree of Life

*I*f there is one central theme in the Zohar—The Book of Brilliance—it is the ongoing drama of reuniting the Divine Feminine with the Divine Masculine. In kabbalistic thinking, the exile of the Shekhinah becomes the metaphor for understanding all forms of disharmony that affect human beings. In repetitive examples, the Kabbalah speaks of the challenges from negative forces to the unity of the divine emanations on the Tree of Life, and it points the way for human prayer and ritual actions to heal the split. What we inherit from the mystical writers of the late medieval period is the beginning of an approach to presenting and interpreting the attributes of God in language that parallels human experience. Structured in terms of the topography of the Tree of Life, the *midot* or attributes of God are mapped out as Sephirot, zones on the tree that each contain a particular vortex of divine energy. Within the tree, all attributes begin with the Ayn Sof Or, the endless light beyond time, space, form, and gender. The Ayn Sof endows Keter, the crown (like the crown chakra), with the great gift of white light, which Keter then shares with the two other Sephirot on the upper triad—Chokhmah (wisdom) and Binah (understanding).

There are three pillars in the system, representing the masculine on the right, the feminine on the left, and the balanced energies in the Middle Pillar. On the upper left is the Upper Mother, Ima, in the Sephira of Binah, the great womb of the cosmos, who gives form to everything and gives birth to the seven lower Sephirot. Below her on the left is Gevurah, who represents the forces of power, law, and justice. Below Gevurah, the feminine energetic is expressed in Hod, translated as "splendor" or "glory." These three and the base of the tree, known as Malkhut, or sovereignty (kingdom, queendom), are the assigned attributes for delineating the various aspects of the Divine Feminine on the tree. The masculine, in the right-hand pillar, is embodied in the upper triad as Chokhmah, the Upper Father of Wisdom, who contains the architectural design of the cosmos. In the next triad, the male Sephira is known as Chesed, or loving kindness. Descending to the next level, we encounter Netzach, translated as "endurance" or "victory." While the Middle Pillar is seen as the unified force field (Keter to Daat, down through Tiferet, Yesod, and Malkhut), it is not gender neutral. Keter, close to the source, is, like its origin, in pure white light. Tiferet is the young male energy, the Kadosh Baruch Hu, the Holy Blessed One. Yesod, in the foundation, is the divine phallus, which holds all the descending energy; and at the base of the tree is Malkhut, the Shekhinah or Daughter, who receives her nourishment from above.

In this system, which was informed by medieval consciousness, the female energy plays a receptive but significant role in the system. It is also seen as the source of negative or demonic energies. While the beginnings of these concepts were already embedded in the older *Sefer Bahir*, which appeared in Europe around the eleventh century (often attributed to the second-century sage Nechunia ben Hakanah), the Zohar, written in the thirteenth century, put these ideas into more explicit literary form, although it never employed visual images, which are prohibited by the Second Commandment.

In their teachings about Binah, the kabbalistic sages seem to have retained a memory or concept of the Mother Goddess in her role as the cosmic womb who gives birth to the galactic universe and all its creatures. In the Jewish system, Chokhmah, the upper male or Divine Father, provides the template for the design of creation—although Chokhmah is a feminine noun, recalling the Wisdom figure described in Proverbs as God's first creation. The plan embedded in Chokhmah cannot be actualized or manifested without the female Binah, who brings the plan to the level of matter and form. Binah, as the Supernal Mother, spreads her wings over the whole world;

she is the source of all souls, who ultimately return to her. Binah is therefore known as *teshuvah*, or repentance/return. During the Jewish High Holy Days, when we ask for teshuvah, we are symbolically asking to return to the Great Mother Binah, the *tsror ha chaim*, the treasure house of all souls.

All the next seven Sephirot—referred to as *sefirei ha binyah*, or the attributes of construction—emanate from Binah and eventually empty into her daughter, Malkhut, the Lower Shekhinah. She who sits at the base of the tree, while owning nothing, takes in the colors and energies from all the vessels who precede her.

The Zohar projects a medieval division of gender characteristics: the male is architectural and generative in Chokhmah; the female is receptive and birth giving in Binah. However, there is respect for the potencies on both the male and female sides of the tree. Binah, characterized as deep understanding, is also the power of speech and sound, which are fundamental to creation. The kabbalistic view is that the world was created with ten great vibrations or sounds, known as *eser maamarot*, which circulated through the cosmos. These are also the sounds that reverberate at Mount Sinai with the giving of the Torah and the inscription of the Ten Commandments. Consistent with this association of the feminine with sound and speech, Shekhinah is identified as *dibbur* or *memra*, translated as "sacred sound." This is a great improvement over the Talmudic notion that women were given a disproportionate allocation of speech! In effect, Binah emanates the inner world of the Godhead and expresses it, for the first time, as an active force. She brings to fruition the seed of divine thought received from her partner. The Upper Father and Mother (Abbah and Ima, that is, Chokhmah and Binah) are united in a permanent connection; they are indivisible and constitute the unswerving nature of God's plan for the universe. Since they are the aspects closest to the crown energy of Keter pouring down from the Ayn Sof Or, there is no duality in their relationship, only divine love and total devotion to the outpouring of God's energy. Some sources portray this as an endless sexual embrace; other references in the Zohar categorize their love as "brotherly." This relationship is in contrast with the ongoing love affair between Tiferet and Malkhut, who are destined to attain union as bride and groom. According to Kabbalah, they are reunited every Sabbath but require help from the human dimension to bring about their permanent sexual reunion, which will ensure the balance of the planet earth.

The Zohar offers occasional surprises in its alignment of qualities with the sexes. In most systems, the Divine Feminine is the source of love and compassion, like the earthly mother. While earlier generations sometimes portrayed Shekhinah as the all-compassionate Mother, in the kabbalistic system of the Zohar, loving kindness, or what we might describe as unconditional love, is assigned to the male in the attribute of Chesed, modeled on the hospitable nature of the patriarch Abraham. The punitive role of avenger and destroyer is ascribed to Gevurah on the left, or female, side of the tree. Like the awesome Hindu goddess Kali, Shekhinah has her moments of expressing divine retribution, especially toward those who have persecuted her treasured people. The Zohar places Shekhinah in charge of the armies of God, as well as the angels, and the midrashic literature cites the role of Shekhinah in punishing the Egyptian armies for their persecution of the Hebrew slaves by drowning the Egyptians in the Red Sea. (Another midrash has God silencing the angels from singing during this terrible event, because the Egyptians are also God's children.) While Shekhinah is considered the mother of all beings, she is also presented as an ethnoparticular goddess who has a special and protective relationship with her people, Israel. In understanding Gevurah as the power of law and order, the mystics are also remembering an ancient view of the goddess in her mighty role as the great judge, carrier of divine fury, and arbiter of life and death. In this conceptual framework, we are led to understand and appreciate the human mother as the chief educator and disciplinarian. The human father in later Chasidic commentary is presented as the embodiment of Chesed, or the indulgent parent whose love for his child overflows into one long and uninterrupted YES!

From this vantage point, we can understand the Gevurah-filled life of the biblical prophet Devorah, who rose to assert herself as Mother in Israel at a time when the tribes needed a strong leader and moral voice. Unwilling to accept the decay of moral values, Devorah spoke truth to power and mobilized an army whose general would not fight without her. According to the Book of Judges, Devorah went on to judge the people for forty years. Later Rabbis would argue about how a woman could be a judge when women could not be witnesses in a court of Jewish law. They decided that she was a prophet moved by the Holy Spirit, asserting her power through prophecy rather than the legal system. This paradox is an example of one that often enters didactic Jewish thinking when discussing the female. This is most striking in the portrayal of Gevurah; her anger is considered the gateway to the demonic, where her counterpart, Lilith, rules with Samael. Shekhinah becomes a captive of the *sitra achra*, or other side, during the weekdays and is estranged from her consort, while all other Sephirot, as midot or attributes of the Divine, stay anchored in their divinity no matter what their function. It is female anger that has the potential to go off course and descend into the demonic netherworld.

As we proceed down the tree into the third triad, the male is empowered thru Netzach, endurance or victory, to carry the vision from Tiferet, beauty or harmony—the young masculine energy—to manifestation. It is considered masculine to struggle and strive toward achievement and victory, while the recipient feminine counterpart, Hod, sits in the place of vision and prophecy, holding the place of prayer and ritual so that the light can radiate in all its glory. With a more neutral view of these midot, we can see the role of Netzach in striving to fulfill the vision seen in Tiferet, and consider Hod to be reverberating the intention and focusing on actualization of the dream. Ultimately, the flow of all energies down the Middle Pillar of the tree, thru Yesod, or foundation—represented by the masculine phallus and the persona of the biblical Joseph—empty into Malkhut, or sovereignty. This is the site of Shekhinah, who is capable of accepting and integrating the flow of colors from all the preceding vessels. Shekhinah then contains all colors that have assembled in the great outpouring of God energy in its descent down the Tree of Life.

Most significant in this flow of energy is the relationship between Tiferet (the son) and Malkhut (the daughter). It is their divine marriage that is constantly sought after in prayer to sustain the life of the world. Tiferet and Malkhut, unlike the Upper Sephirot, are caught up in the drama of glorious unification, followed by abject separation. They represent paradise and exile. Like human lovers, they have many ups and downs and experience many setbacks on the road to a repaired or Messianic world. In the kabbalistic scheme of things, human beings are here to help reunite these archetypal representatives of the *shevira*—the breakage that took place when God's energy began to flow into the vessels of creation. According to the sixteenth-century saint Rabbi Isaac Luria (known as Ari, the lion), this model of breakage, called shevira and *tikkun* (repair), is the basic model directing human efforts in the world. Given that philosophy, all blessings among the sixteenth-century Lurianic circle of kabbalistic practitioners, influenced by the work of Rabbi Moses Cordovero, began with the Aramaic invocation "L shem yichud kudsha b'rich hu u'shekhinteh," which translates, For the sake of the unification of the Kadosh Baruch Hu [God's name in Tiferet, the Holy Blessed One] and his Shekhinah [the name for God's energy in Malkhut]. According to this circle of practitioners, which included the great scholars Rabbi Cordovero, Rabbi Chaim Vital, and other luminaries, the Shabbat rituals and prayers, including lovemaking, were designed to accelerate that process of reunification. All the mitzvot would hasten the coming together of these realms in a weekly hieros gamos, sacred marriage. Prayers and intentions would release the Shekhinah from her captivity. Like the princess abducted by the demons, or the rose surrounded by thorns, she was seen as being trapped among the powers of evil during the week. Conversely, negative deeds could widen the chasm between the divine pair. Traditional Jewish liturgy for receiving the Sabbath still includes the "L'cha Dodi" (Come My

Beloved) poem addressed to Shekhinah, written by Rabbi Shlomo Alkabetz in sixteenth-century S'fat in northern Israel. It is still sung every Friday night in synagogues around the world. Home practice includes the beautiful erotic poetry of the Song of Songs, and the Eyshet Chayil prayer praising the righteous wife, who represents Shekhinah in the domestic realm.

For that generation of kabbalistic adepts in the circle of the Ari, envisioning or hearing the Shekhinah was a very important component in the spiritual quest of the disciple. Most outstanding in this realm is the role of Rabbi Joseph Caro, a learned rabbi and jurist of Turkish background known for his authorship of the *Shulchan Aruch*, the major compendium of Jewish law. Caro was known to receive direction and guidance from a heavenly *maggid,* or guide, who was identified with the Shekhinah and the Mishnah. According to Caro's biographer, Zvi Verblosky, Rabbi Caro shared his channeling with his students on Friday nights, speaking in a deep feminine voice, which he associated with the Shekhinah.

Another classic example from that circle of seeking the Shekhinah in vision is conveyed in a story about Rabbi Abraham ha Levi of S'fat, who was eager for a vision of Shekhinah (reported in *Jewish Mystical Testimonies* by Rabbi Lewis Jacobs *z"l* ). Rabbi Abraham was sent to Jerusalem, a difficult trip at that time, by his master, the Ari. When he saw the deteriorated nature of the holy city, he wept and hit his head on the stones, resulting in loss of consciousness. In that altered state he experienced the Shekhinah as Mother Zion, the mourning crone, draped in black and still bewailing the loss of Beit ha Mikdash, her holy temple, and the exile of her treasured people. (Shekhinah was considered the mistress of the temple, and the divine abode is an expression of her abounding love.) In effect, this part of Rabbi Abraham's vision was a continuation of the vision of the prophet Jeremiah, who also saw Mother Zion draped in black and weeping for the loss of the temple. The other side of Reb Abraham's vision involved the appearance of the consoling Shekhinah, who put her hand on his face and wiped away his tears, reassuring him in the language of Jeremiah's vision of

Rachel, "There is hope for the future, and your children will be returned to their borders" (Jer. 31:14–17).

In other narratives, Shekhinah is a beautiful young woman, adorned with precious gems and draped in exquisite clothing, perhaps representing the younger version of Shekhinah as *betulah*, or virgin, daughter of the King of Kings. This form is more reminiscent of the visions among the Merkavah mystics, in which the radiant Shekhinah, queen of the seven heavens, appears at the end of the adept's journey, adorned with the most luxurious fabrics and gemstones. Seated at the *kisei ha kavod* (throne of glory), she is the ultimate splendor, the Divine Glory of the higher realms, called ziv ha Shekhinah, so radiant that the angels must cover their eyes. The seeming paradox of Shekhinah as mourning crone and gorgeous maiden makes sense when it is subsumed in the mythical context of female as maiden, woman, and crone. The Shabbos Queen, who is Mother, or Matrona, provides the context for the midlife female. In Eyshet Chayil (Woman of Valor), the Friday night ode that the husband is supposed to recite to his wife, she is praised as the industrious organizer of family life—the center of this three-part goddess triumvirate. As Binah, she is celebrated as the Supernal Mother who watches over all creation, waiting for us to return to her in our final merger with the light.

There are scholars who portray the reunification of the Upper and Lower Shekhinah, exemplified by Leah and Rachel, as the most important *yichud*, or unification, for the salvation of the planet. This metaphoric emphasis on reuniting the Upper and Lower Mothers (Binah and Malkhut) offers an alternative, perhaps same-sex, approach to rebalancing the planet, focusing on the importance of the mother-daughter relationship among human beings. The Upper and Lower Mothers occupy very different realms, and their distance from each other on the tree makes for a more challenging, long-distance relationship. For all beings, the teshuvah (return) to Binah is the goal of life, but it is difficult to carry out because of all the distractions at the earthly level.

# Kabbalah

The missing element in this brilliant system is, of course, the participation of women. All our information is based on the literature of male writers, subsumed in a male-centered religious culture. Occasionally we get a biography or journal that gives us more insight into the contributions of specific women, usually those outstanding in wealth and social status. For example, the great Portuguese philanthropist Doña Gracia Nasi (1510–70) supported kabbalistic scholars in northern Israel through both charity and employment. Her contact with Joseph Caro is documented; he sat as a judge on a *beit din* (religious court) in a fiscal suit she was involved in that took place in Constantinople, Turkey. Doña Gracia purchased the land grant for all the land from Tiberias to S'fat from the sultan of Turkey, with the intent of developing a sustainable environment for Jews coming to the Holy Land from Europe. Her charities extended to many in Israel, as they did in Turkey and western Europe—typically schools, hospitals, and synagogues. We also know from the newly translated journals of Chaim Vital that there were female intuitives who were highly regarded by the community. The piety of women in such roles would be a given. Considering the mystical focus on reincarnation, known as *gilgul*, it is not surprising that these scholars speculated on the past lives of their wives. In fact, Moshe Chaim Luzzatto, the famous Italian mystic, believed that his wife was the reincarnation of the biblical Tziporah, just as he was supposedly the embodiment of the prophet Moses!

The Zohar considers women to have an inherent connection with Shekhinah. In fact, men are supposed to marry so that they can have their connection to the Divine Presence assured through their wives. In effect, the kabbalistic attitude suggests that women receive their spiritual energy biologically, with only a few religious ritual obligations. Men, on the other hand, are required to work at it, with devotion, ritual, and prayer three times a day. For the mystics of Sephardic background, there was also an element of chivalry built into the system. In S'fat on Friday night, after welcoming the Shekhinah outdoors in the hills, the men would come home and kiss the hand of the woman of the house, who had prepared the home and the celebratory Friday night meal honoring the weekly return of the Shekhinah. A special *kiddush* for sanctification over the wine and food entitled "Atkeenu seudata d' atika kadisha" (I will prepare the meal of perfect faith for the Holy Ancient One) was written by the Ari for each of the Shabbat meals. The Zohar goes into great detail on the spiritual meaning of each special meal or *seudah,* indicating that the Friday night meal is specifically designated for welcoming Shekhinah, who is the spirit and Queen of the Sabbath, bringing with her angels who usher in Sabbath peace and rest from all conflict.

# *Meditation*
## Entering the Tree of Life

The Zohar, the Book of Brilliance, and the kabbalistic literature that followed gave us a wonderful model for understanding how God's attributes, the midot, come forth from the Tree of Life, expressed through the Adam Kadmon, a primordial human archetype. We can therefore approach the Sephirot through our own physical bodies, which encompass the balance between the divine feminine and the divine masculine energies.

Come with me now on a journey through the Sephirot on the Tree of Life. Imagine that from the Ayn Sof Or, the endless light of the formless God, there is a narrow beam of white light descending directly into the top of your head, into Keter, the crown or crown chakra. That light then descends into the right temple corresponding to the attribute called Chokhmah, or wisdom, identified as the Upper Father, in which is encoded the architectural design of the universe. These components are present and waiting to be activated by Binah, the Upper Mother. Chokhmah sends the light energy across to the left temple, into the realm of Binah, the Upper Mother or Upper

Shekhinah, the great womb of all the worlds. Binah can give form to every-thing, and proceeds to pour out the galaxies, the planets, the stars, the hu-mans, the animals. In this upper triangle of divine energy, we already have the beginning of creation.

But by itself up there, the energy is too remote; it must descend so it can be utilized. It comes down through the Middle Pillar, spiraling through the center of the cranium, behind the eyes and nose, into the throat, home of all music. It is as if it has crossed a frontier (known as Daat) and is now entering a different zone—the arena of human emotion.

This stream of light now travels across the right shoulder, down the right arm—identified as the masculine side—and into the right hand. There it becomes the giving energy, known as Chesed, loving kindness, unconditional love. Again, the moving energy seeks its partner, its balance. So imagine that energy now traveling across the shoulder blades to the left shoulder, then down the left arm into the left hand. This area, considered the restrainer, is known as Gevurah, the source of *din,* or judgment, where the mother has to say, "This is not good for you. There have to be rules; there have to be bound-aries." And so these two parts, Chesed and Gevurah, are the elements that come together and unite in the heart, where the energy of Tiferet—golden, young masculine energy of beauty and love—resides. Imagine a line from each side, right and left joining together in your heart space. Let yourself feel this process of emotional balance.

We are now in the second descending triangle, which is about how we manage many of our relationships. And since this too is not yet complete, the stream of energy now travels into the right hip, the place of Netzach, perseverance, endurance, winning, ultimately victory. That active mascu-line energy is needed to accomplish things in the world, to put ideas for-ward and make our dreams a reality. You might put your right foot forward and remind yourself of how you feel when you are determined to complete something important. When you have enough experience of that feeling, let the energy travel to the left hip, which is Netzach's true partner. This Sephira is known as Hod, the feminine splendor, where we can appreciate all that has transpired, and all the effort we have put in. In Hod, we are in the place of actualization, where the goal reverberates into a state of being.

When Netzach and Hod are in balance, their energies descend into the pubic triangle, into Yesod, the genital foundation of productivity, life, and holiness. Yesod, like a dam, holds everything for a while, containing these qualities that make up the third descending triangle, which is the triad of governance. But Yesod cannot ultimately hold all this light of many colors and many forms, so it releases them into the earth, into Malkhut, to the Lower Shekhinah, who is connected to the animals, plants, stones, and human beings. Our feet can be in relationship with this Divine Presence who makes herself felt in the earth—she who is available to us, the very closest quality of the source energy.*

Now you can experience yourself as a light being who is the connector between heaven and earth, and who carries Shekhinah's energy everywhere. Everywhere you go and for everyone you meet, may you be the blessing. May you be the light carrier.

---

* If you wish to reverse this process, you can imagine this energy coming up from Malkhut, rising up through the feet, ascending through the legs and hips and up into the heart, the shoulders, the arms, and back up out the top of the head.

Part 2

---

*Holding Her Place*

*On this Sabbath night this supernal point* [Shekhinah] *spreads forth light, spreading her wings over the world. All other dominions pass away. The world grows secure.*

—Elliot Ginsburg

*The Supernal Holy One* [Shekhinah] *descends and spreads her wings over Israel, sheltering them as a mother bird does her fledglings. . . . As* [Shekhinah] *hovers over them, wings outstretched over her children, She brings forth new souls for each and every person.*

—Elliot Ginsburg

*This tabernacle of peace* [Sabbath] *is the Matron of the world. Hence it behooves the matron to kindle the light . . . because thereby she is attaching herself to her rightful place.*

—Zohar

*Ribono Shel Olam* [Master of the World], *may my mitzvah of lighting candles be accepted in the way the mitzvah of the high Priest was accepted when he lit the Menorah in the beloved Holy Temple.*

—Sarah Bas Tovim

*For the Sabbath is a Queen and a Bride.*

—Zohar

# Chapter 8

# Shabbos Queen
## Celebrating through History

The Jewish observance of the Sabbath on the sacred seventh day goes back to Genesis, with the Creator resting after the six great "days" of creation (in Jewish commentaries, these "days" are regarded as epochs, extending over vast amounts of time). The Torah's instructions for remembering and guarding the Sabbath come from Exodus, as part of the Decalogue received at Mount Sinai. The Sabbath is fundamental to the Mosaic religious code, imparted over the generations as a way of living in alignment with the original cosmic rhythm. Celebration in ancient times revolved around the cessation of work, commemorating freedom from Egyptian bondage and loyalty to the redemptive God force.

That process of setting aside "sacred time" became even more critical when the Israelites were exiled from their country. On their own land, the cohesiveness of national identity had been reinforced by the monarchy and the central temple worship in Jerusalem. The Babylonian exile was the first in many major events that would lead to the Sabbath becoming a defining feature of Jewish life, in effect setting Jewish communities apart from their neighbors. While Christian and Islamic Sabbaths are both patterned on the Jewish Shabbat, they were moved to different days to commemorate events in the newer religions and to separate them from their origin. By the beginning of the Common Era, the Sabbath had become the central practice for Jewish communities in both Israel and the Diaspora. Specific customs and prayers for creating sacred time through observance of Sabbath rest and delight were spelled out by later generations of rabbis. The Talmud details the thirty-nine prohibited forms of work; these were drawn from the description in the Torah of the various tasks performed in the construction of the Tabernacle in the wilderness, described in Exodus 31 and spelled out in Mishnah Shabbat 7:2.

The holiness of the day was not just a function of rest, family time, and communal worship; it also involved the special Sabbath liturgy and three celebratory meals. Torah study and other devotions were always emphasized, leading to the creation of a *mikdash m'at* (miniature sanctuary) in the home. These portable sanctuaries were carried around the planet by the exiled Israelites and protected from workaday concerns by a code of speech, thought, and behavior that informed the Sabbath atmosphere for generations of observant Jews around the globe.

Even in early texts, the Sabbath was portrayed as bride and queen coming from the divine world. However, the development of that concept and its connection with the feminine Shekhinah became far more elaborate in kabbalistic thinking. The early medieval Jewish philosophers had stressed the restorative power of the Sabbath and its healing light through opportunities for leisure and intellectual exchange (the latter shared mostly by men), which would have been welcome in a preindustrial era in which most creative efforts were labor intensive. Yehudah Ha Levi (1080–1141), one of the great poetic voices of the Sephardic world, wrote in his epic philosophical work, *The Kuzari*, of the "spiritual fullness and communion with the Divine" that entered with the holy Sabbath. Those ideas continued developing and came to fullness with the emergence of the Zohar. In mapping out the location of the Shekhinah, as the Sabbath, in Malkhut on the Tree of Life, the early Kabbalists opened the gateway to intensified experience of the Divine Presence on Sabbath, as well as on holidays and New Moon, focusing on feeling God's presence in the roots of the Tree of Life, close to human physicality. The Zohar goes into great detail about the logistics of Sabbath preparation and inviting Shekhinah in through the aesthetic of cleanliness and beauty of the household. The beds are supposed to be made and the pillows plumped up! The scene for welcoming the Divine Presence also includes special food, good wine, music and prayer, and the focus on love between marriage partners, friends, and family. While that attribute of love is always present, it can find greater expression on the Sabbath when there is a cessation of outside activities. In kabbalistic thinking, the Sabbath provided the opportunity to live out and perform the mitzvot that would harmonize the planet and unite the cosmic lovers represented by Malkhut and Tiferet. The adept would be going from theory to practice on Shabbos, enacting in his marital life the conjugal theme that he was studying in the Zohar during the week. Making love to his wife on the Sabbath, he and his partner could become the facilitators for the sacred marriage that was taking place above. In effect, Shabbat inside the Tree of Life provided the basis for a Jewish tantra for those who were knowledgeable and observant. We do not know if these ideas and practices of the Spanish and French mystics extended to the less educated (nor do we know about the female experience, though we would hope that such an elevated philosophy would have led to a beautiful sex life for the wives of mystics) or to Jewish communities in other parts of the world. For example, the Ethiopian Jews, known as Beta Yisrael, have the concept of Shekhinah and are very Sabbath observant, even though they did not have the same literature as the European Jews.

We do know that the next wave of great kabbalistic practitioners in the circle of the Rabbi Isaac Luria in sixteenth-century S'fat in northern Israel was aligned with the Shabbat philosophy expressed in the Zohar and the commentaries that followed. Many of the teachers in the S'fat circle who came from Sephardic backgrounds were *m'kubalim* (initiates in the mystical tradition) and considered themselves inheritors and disseminators of the kabbalistic wisdom they had received. Their small, tight-knit, and very observant community became a living laboratory for creating the mystical Sabbath others dreamed of. Collective adherence to Halakhah created the atmosphere for profound Sabbath observance, grounded in regular meetings of the community to share in practices for reinforcing and enhancing observance. History records that town criers circulated in the neighborhoods to announce the coming of the Sabbath, so that householders would put out their fires on time.

The saintly teachers of the community, who spent many hours together in meditation and prayer during the week, gathered on Friday afternoons with their disciples after immersing in a special mikveh and went out into the hills to sing and welcome the Shekhinah. From that circle we have the "L'cha Dodi" (Come My Beloved) prayer. These Kabbalists believed that women had an inherent connection with Shekhinah, and that men were able to receive the Divine Presence through their wives. Given that view, the sexual relationship took on special significance, especially on the Sabbath, when they were expected to give their wives pleasure. They would also circumambulate the dining room table seven times. This practice emanated from the teaching that since the destruction of the temple, the Sabbath table became the substitute for the temple's holy sacrificial altar. That belief would certainly have placed value on the woman's work to create the special Sabbath meals, in addition to separation of challah, immersion in mikveh, and candle lighting.

Since most of the old synagogues in S'fat have women's galleries, women clearly attended services and were probably familiar with the liturgy, as well as with Sabbath customs. Little has been written on the education of the women of that period, but the daughters of scholarly Sephardic families were most likely to have been educated in the Hebrew liturgy. There were also many prayers and devotional songs composed in Ladino (Judeo-Spanish) that the women would have known. While the S'fat experience stands out as a kind of laboratory in intense mystical Judaism, it had a short life historically due to adverse living conditions in the Holy Land.

While the tradition of venerating the Shabbat as queen and bride was celebrated everywhere Jews lived, each area of the world tended to retain some customs that reflected its culture, especially in musical melodies and food. Most sang the full "L'cha Dodi" on Friday nights and read the Eyshet Chayil and the Song of Songs. East and west, men prepared the candles or oil wicks for the woman of the house, acknowledging the role of the woman as the conduit for the entry of the Sabbath. The tradition of baking twelve small loaves of bread or rolls, symbolizing the tribes, was popular in the Middle East and Europe. Also widespread was the custom of eating fish on Shabbat, based on the assumption that the souls of the righteous are reincarnated in fish. The frenetic preparation to complete shopping, cooking, and cleaning before the Sabbath (still apparent in Israel and Orthodox communities everywhere) was a fact of life for all who were observant.

The next wave of mystics who welcomed the Shabbos Queen with ecstatic music and dance, believing that they could bring the Divine Presence back to earth, were the great *tsaddikim* who headed the Chasidic courts of eastern Europe. These courts, which often became family dynasties, were like Hindu ashrams, where devotees could be with their holy teachers and like-minded believers. All were welcomed into study and prayer, meditation and music, counsel and healing. Devotees participated in communal meals and were made to feel they had a spiritual home. Some courts were simple and small in scale; others were large and elegant. The early leaders of the eighteenth century, including the Baal Shem Tov, were very familiar with the kabbalistic texts as well as more traditional Jewish study of Torah, Talmud, and Gemara. Because the Chasidim emphasized communal participation even of the least literate, they have been regarded as less studious than their more rationalistic counterparts, called *mitnadgim*, who opposed the flexibility of Chasidic customs. While Chasidim too trained their closest disciples to be like knights who could redeem the Shekhinah from her exile, they spoke of the Shekhinah resting on people's faces, especially those of pious women. However, these early teachers and saints did not emerge until after the Chmelnitsky pogroms in the mid-1600s, which killed one third of the Jewish population in Europe. European Jewry was also still recovering from a crisis within Judaism known as the Sabbatean heresy, in which huge numbers of Jews became followers of the charismatic Shabbtai Tsvi (1626–76), who had declared himself the Messiah. The disillusionment following his downfall had a significant effect on ensuing generations of Jewish teachers, which probably led them to deemphasize the esoteric and erotic aspects of the Kabbalah in favor of a more grounded practice of Judaism. The early Chasidic teachers were eager to provide a period of both piety and a sense of greater security to their flocks, who tended to be drawn from the poor. To people in difficult circumstances with limited resources, the Sabbath was indeed like paradise. Once a week they could rest in the sanctuary of time with the Shabbos Queen. All issues of poverty, illness, and suffering were suspended on Friday night, when the Shekhinah was released from her captivity by the negative forces for the celebration of hope and a liberated future.

In effect, the kabbalistic notion of an imprisoned Shekhinah taken over by foreign forces of evil was an apt metaphor for their own lives. The eastern European Jewish communities were largely alienated from the religions and cultures that surrounded them, in contrast to those in Italy and western Europe of that period, where Jews—though different because of their religious observance—were more a part of the larger society. In the Middle East, Jewish practice was closer to Islam, and the population was not as frequently attacked and displaced.

While persecution continually threatened the provincial eastern European Jews, they also enjoyed the leadership of illuminated saints who helped sustain their belief system. The blessing of being around the enlightened tsaddik served to reinforce the communal sharing of Sabbath customs and the sense of Shekhinah's protection. The piety generated by the Chasidic movement, though based on strict adherence to religious law, was joyous, emphasizing music and dance to bring worshippers to states of ecstasy. In that environment, observing the mitzvot and Shabbat would have felt like a guarantee that the Divine Presence would watch over her children, the people of Israel, and eventually punish all those who persecuted them.

The essential Sabbath rituals in the home continued to be the province of women. The tekhinot, prayers created for and mostly by women, were usually written in Yiddish because the female population was not literate in Hebrew. Those prayers reflect an awareness of the larger cosmic role that was the basis of domestic rituals. The Chasidic leaders recognized the holiness and prophetic abilities of women, acknowledging women in their families for their healing and intuitive skills and honoring them as women of wisdom who offered counsel and advice to the community. While early Chasidism may have had some egalitarian components, the times did not allow for a major opening for women. Many women saints of the time were recognized, but probably perceived as yotseit min ha klal (the exception that proves the rule), thus their example could not mobilize women for greater gender equity—similar, perhaps, to India, where women saints were revered, but ordinary women continued to be subject to widespread discrimination.

Although drawn from the esoteric storehouse of Zoharic writing and popularized by mystics and Chasidim, welcoming the Sabbath remained an important part of Jewish life, reflected in the poetry of the Haskalah writers. In the twentieth century, the beauty of the Sabbath permeated kibbutz life in Israel, involving even the more secular intentional communities. In Israel, as the Sabbath descends, transportation and commerce cease. The sense of shifting time is unique and palpable for everyone in the country. Observant Jews feel that the people of Israel around the world become more united, despite their differences, in a weekly harmonic convergence. In that vibratory communion, there is an open channel to Shekhinah, with prayers for life and love and family. It is the appropriate time to ask for health and peace and prosperity for all the world. Ushering in Shabbat rest is one of the regular times in the life of the Jewish woman when she becomes priestess, ritual leader, and vessel for the sacred energy. An eighteenth-century *tekhinah* has the woman telling God that she has become like the high priest in the Holy Temple.

In the modern era, this memory of the mother of the house as preserver of tradition is also linked with popular notions of provincial eastern European life that have been romanticized in films and literature, perhaps from the desire to imagine a simpler time in which family and community were more intact. (Interestingly, the women writers of twentieth-century Israel do not portray their mothers nostalgically.) The glue for all Jewish life has always been the women whose devoted work in the household made possible the celebration of Shabbat and holidays and the handing down of customs from one generation to another. Since Judaism is a householder's religion, the labor-intensive support system that underlies the Shabbat and the holidays was always the province of women.

Among contemporary Jewish women, few bake their own challah, and only a small minority use the mikveh and observe the Jewish sexual codes. Hence, the lighting of the Shabbat candles remains the single most widespread female mitzvah. I have led Kabbalat Shabbat and Rosh Chodesh groups in which candle lighting took up much of the evening and involved the sharing of blessings and profound insights. For it is in the silent entry of Shekhinah at that time that the Sabbath can begin. This is the critical juncture, the place of the shifting energy and the beginning of the sacred marriage. *Hadlakat nerot* (candle lighting) is a popular theme in Jewish art for good reason. In my experience, it is one of the indelible memories that many older Jews carry that links them to the tradition through their feminine ancestors. For men particularly, these memories of mother and grandmother at the Shabbat table is one of the strongest places of awareness of the Divine Feminine. For women, the act itself is one of induction into priestess consciousness. Taking on this ceremonial act is often the gateway to stronger observance. In this regard, all streams of Judaism agree in trying to recruit participation in the very fundamental rites of weekly Shabbat practice as a first step toward deeper involvement in the spiritual path.

The veneration of the Sabbath as queen and bride was retained by Jewish communities around the world and is still sustained, especially in Friday night services, when it is traditional to stand for the entry of the Shekhinah with the singing of the last stanza of "L'cha Dodi." I suspect that the tradition of standing up for the bride at weddings may have originated in the recognition of Shekhinah in all brides. While viewpoints differ among the various streams of Judaism on other issues, there is general agreement about the centrality of welcoming the Shekhinah and creating the special atmosphere of the Sabbath, with the prayers and songs that are intoned on the day of rest.

# *Meditation*
## Welcoming the Sabbath Queen

It is Friday afternoon, and you are eager to complete your work for the week. You have answered all your e-mail, returned phone calls, and reached a good stopping point with all your projects. You straighten up your office and prepare to leave the workweek behind.

Today you are going for a special mikveh ritual in a river. You might visualize yourself with a partner, your best friend, or some very good friends. You have heard about this lovely spot where there is a pool of water secluded from sight where you can bathe in the nude. You take a ride in the country, and soon you are in a wooded area that surrounds the pristine water. You are delighted that it is not freezing cold, but definitely refreshing. You and your friends hang your clothes on a nearby tree, and together you intone the Shehechianu prayer for first-time events. You talk about the things in your daily life that you would like to release to the water and send back to the Divine Mother. Each of you has a spirit buddy who will watch to assure that your immersion is total. You have prepared yourself by removing all jewelry so you enter the water pure and simple, as you entered the world. You walk out to where it is deep enough for complete immersion. You share a song about the waters of redemption, and then you each articulate the blessing thanking the Divine for this ritual. Now it is time to let

# Chapter 8

go, to invite Shekhinah to carry away all your cares and responsibilities. You go under the water fully three times, visualizing all that you are releasing, and then you decide on a fourth descent to bring in the healing energies. Feeling both chilled and energized, you run out of the river, eager to put on the clean white clothes you brought with you. You are all laughing and happy, feeling as if you have given birth to some new part of yourselves.

As you and your friends walk on the beautiful path around the water, you sense the presence of the Divine all around you. You feel loved and supported by the universe, free of all your usual concerns. You have been invited to a special Sabbath dinner with friends who live near the river. You see that the sun is beginning to descend, and you are glad that you will be lighting the Sabbath candles just on time. You are welcomed into their home, where the table is already set with an elegant white cloth and their best dishes. You admire the beautiful candlesticks and special beeswax candles and enjoy the painted silk cover over the two large challah breads. The very best kosher wines are arrayed on the sideboard, as well as organic grape juice. Exquisitely arranged vases of fragrant flowers adorn the room, and the entire house reflects devotion to cleanliness and beauty. You are so happy to be with these friends who share your devotion to Sabbath preparation.

As sunset approaches, you share songs welcoming Shekhinah's presence, and then you close your eyes, intone the blessing, and light the candles. Making the three circuits around the light with your hands, you understand that you can reach the circles of souls in your life, your community, and around the world. The tapers light up the faces of all present, and you notice the blissful moment when Shekhinah enters and you experience inner light and warmth all around you. Infused with love, you know you can send blessings to others, anywhere. You visualize friends and relatives and send them your good thoughts. You can also feel the spirits of loved ones who have crossed over sending you their blessings. One of the friends is giving his child the priestly benediction, and it becomes a blessing of protection for children everywhere. In the sublime stillness that follows, you all sit and meditate, understanding the harmony of all beings and planets on this holy night. You enter a timeless world beyond war and famine, greed and envy, in which past, present, and future become one.

Now it is time to bless the wine and the bread. You lift the special kiddush cup and sing the prayer, radiating it to your friends and loved ones as a ritual of initiation into the mystery of the vine. One of the group reads from the Song of Songs, and the words burst into meaning within your mind and heart. This wine is the elixir of unconditional love for all beings. This bread has braided into it the secrets of the universe. Even one taste can transform consciousness. As the rich Sabbath bread is placed in your mouth, you feel the molecules of wheat lighting up all your cells. You are shifting from the dense physical body into a being of light.

You are a being of love, surrounded by the Sabbath angels and ready to enter the Sacred Marriage, whether it is expressed as unifying the disparate parts of your self, making love with your ideal partner, or merging in unconditional love with all beings. Shabbat Shalom!

*It is the Tsaddik sitting in this world gaining merit for himself that may constitute the place where the Shekhinah dwells and upon whom all the good things descend.*

—Moshe Idel

*Think yourself as nothing, and totally forget yourself when you pray. Only have in mind that you are praying for the Divine Presence.*

—Rabbi Dov Baer, Maggid of Mezeritch

*Only the prayer that takes place for the sake of the Shekhinah truly lives.*

—Baal Shem Tov

*Understand that just as you look at physical objects, you must also look with your mind's eye at the Shekhinah. She is forever with you.*

—Rabbi Dov Baer, Maggid of Mezeritch

# Chapter 9

# *Early Chasidism*
## Shekhinah's Return to Humanity

*I*n an era distinguished by the proliferation of great saints, European Chasidism brought the Shekhinah back to the earth embodied in the actions and charismatic personalities of the saints called tsaddikim. These were learned rabbis who embodied the holiness of the Law in their loving personalities and their extraordinary capacity to serve others. The tsaddikim were perceived to experience a special state of transparency that enabled the Shekhinah to live within and through them. Their holiness was cultivated by living in a state of profound humility with devotion to spiritual purity, Torah observance, study, and prayer. Tsaddikim were believed to ascend to the higher realms of *devekut* (attachment to the Divine), which enabled them see into people's souls and do miracles. They also had to be committed to sharing the benefits of that connection with the community. All the issues of daily life fell within the tsaddik's orbit. In that respect, the early leaders of Chasidism, including the Baal Shem Tov and the Maggid of Mezeritch, set a different course from that of their kabbalistic predecessors. They trained their numerous students to concern themselves with the needs of the people and use their spiritual gifts to provide a better life for all. Caring for the poor, elderly, and infirm became a regular part of life in the Chasidic court. Many of the ritual details were handled by male assistants, and it is quite probable that the women took charge of preparing the food and caring for the sick. The life within a Chasidic court resembled that of a Hindu ashram, where the guru graced with the capacity to enter higher states spends much of his or her time providing for the material and emotional welfare of the devotees. Likewise in Judaism, generations of mystics have gone into silence and isolation only to return to deal with the daily concerns of their own families and their followers. Since Judaism lacks a monastic tradition, the saint always had the responsibility of his own marriage and children.

Contact with the tsaddik who embodied the Divine Presence thus became a goal for every devotee. Basking in the illuminated state of these miracle-working rabbis, ordinary Jews might imagine the Shekhinah's presence becoming available to all of them through the blessings of their leaders. Seeking personal audiences for spiritual counseling and guidance was very important. Numerous stories abound crediting the great rebbes of Chasidism with amazing intuitive powers, like their kabbalistic antecedents. The best known of the early tsaddikim was the Baal Shem Tov (1698–1760; Master of the Divine Name), whose life of good works and miracles has been celebrated in stories for hundreds of years. Rabbi Israel ben Eliezer (1698–1760), often referred to by his acronym, the Besht, was reputed to have the capacity to see into the individual's soul and find the exact course he or she needed to follow to do *tikkun nefesh* (repair work for the soul). The Besht is also known for recognizing the intuitive abilities of women, including those of his own daughter, Edel.

In song and dance, the community welcomed Shekhinah weekly as Shabbos Queen and Bride and expanded that worship in lengthy Saturday morning prayers. The joyous *seudah shelishit* (third meal of the Sabbath) was prominent among the Chasidic lineages, where teaching and celebration were connected with concept of Shekhinah being totally present on late Saturday afternoon. Although only men could share food and teachings at the rebbe's *tish* (table) during the Sabbath and holidays, women may have had some ways of participating in the events.

Chasidic practice also popularized the Saturday night Melave Malka ceremony of escorting the queen out of our earthly dimension. The focus on music and dancing, based on the view that sound can become a vessel for the Divine Presence, democratized the rituals so that even the less educated could take part in accompanying the Shekhinah. While the *chevrayah* (companions) of Shekhinah were portrayed as few in earlier centuries, Chasidism emphasized the role of the community in the practice, recognizing that the devotion and enthusiasm of the followers energized the saint and sustained his ability to serve. In their prayers and actions, all male devotees could participate in the great mystery of uniting the Holy Blessed One and Shekhinah. In this way, the Baal Shem and his disciples brought the insights of the Kabbalah to the wider circle of the people. Their practice de-emphasized the powerful erotic components of earlier mystical thought and focused more on living the righteous life.

Devotion in all of daily life was the message brought by the great Chasidic masters. The Baal Shem was known for teaching simply, through parables and stories, bringing the esoteric teachings to the followers in a more user-friendly fashion. Unlike their kabbalistic predecessors, who contemplated the attributes of God in small, elitist rabbinical circles, the Chasidim lived out the belief that Shekhinah rested on the faces of righteous women and men regardless of education or socioeconomic status. Early Chasidism's emphasis on praying with feeling and intentionality *(kavannah)* acknowledged the presence of the Shekhinah even in the prayers of the most uneducated devotee. This attitude, which is reflected in the numerous folk tales in which the prayer ascends through the actions of a child or layperson, might have provided entry for women into the arena of communal Jewish prayer. The rebbe's interest in herbal remedies could have legitimized the herbal knowledge of women; the Besht is said to have learned about herbs from women healers in the Carpathian mountains. Revived focus on dreams would certainly provide an opening for the feminine. The rebbe's emphasis on the importance and magic of food made women, who did the cooking and distributed food to the poor, an important part of the charity system. Unfortunately, it was still a system in which male devotees, as they had been among the Kabbalists, were the chief players in synagogue life and in the cosmic drama of restoring the Shekhinah to the earth. In its creativity and challenge to religious rigidity, Chasidism represented a potential opening of the gates of equality. However, attacks on the movement from established Jewish circles limited radical change, and social conditions in eastern Europe worked against it.

While Jewish women were not yet organized or educated, early Chasidism produced a number of extraordinary women teachers and saints. Most of these figures—whom I like to think of as messengers of the Shekhinah—came from the families of the great rebbes, where they were educated religiously and valued for their wisdom and insight. In the early days, when groups were informal, there may have been more openness to their participation, though it is unlikely that men and women would have stood alongside each other in prayer groups. It is said that Edel, the Baal Shem's saintly daughter, was always "at his side" and available to advise his followers, although it is not clear whether she counseled women only, or both men and women.

There are stories that after the death of her father, no family wedding could begin without her presence and approval. These stories refer as well to her ability to communicate with him in the other world. In the circle of the Baal Shem, devotees described Edel by saying, "The Shekhinah sits on her face." She traveled with the Besht on his attempted journey to Israel and other trips, and cared for him in his later years. Edel's daughter Feige, who was the mother of Rebbe Nachman of Bratslav, was also considered a *tsaddeket* (female saint). The family custom of valuing the insights of women was continued at the table of Feige's brother, Rabbi Baruch of Medzeboz (the Baal Shem's grandson and Edel's second son), where his wife and daughters would join in Torah conversations. In fact, Reb Baruch was criticized for that practice by the Seer of Lublin, one of the most respected religious leaders of that time.

The great Maggid of Mezeritch, who further developed and continued the Chasidic path after the Besht's death, recognized the piety and exceptional intuitive abilities of his daughter-in-law (she has no first name in stories about her; she is sometimes referred to as "daughter of heaven"). According to folktales, she intervened with the heavenly court and managed to extend the life of her ascetic husband, known as Abraham the Angel, the Maggid's only child. She is said to have continued communicating with both Abraham and the Maggid even after their deaths. The disciples of the Maggid also had daughters and mothers who were recognized for their learning, charitable works, and ability to draw down the Ruach ha Kodesh. These women included Freda Zalman's, the daughter of Rabbi Schneur Zalman of Liadi, the founder of Chabad Chasidism. Freda also wrote tracts on religious subjects.

Another heroine of that time is a woman referred to as the mother of Rabbi Leib Soreh's (Rabbi Leib, the son of Soreh). A redeemer of political prisoners, he was named as his mother's son in recognition of his saintly mother's spirituality and courage.

While most of these messengers of Shekhinah did their work quietly, like the "daughter of heaven," others took on more public roles, and some even assumed leadership of their own courts. In this genre is Malka die Triskerin, who was descended from the Chernobyl dynasty. She took on the role of rebbe, receiving petitioners for counseling and feeding the poor of her area on a grand scale twice a day. Little has been written about the daughter of the Rebbe of Trisk (her father was one of the eight sons of the Chernobyl Rebbe), so we have no information on whether she led public prayers or left that to the men. It is known that she loved music and hosted elegant Passover Seders. We have more data about the life of the nineteenth-century tsaddeket Malka of Belz. Malka, a powerful channeler and healer, is credited with being able to intervene with the heavenly court to avert disasters. She supervised food for the poor and incorporated her premonitory knowledge into activities connected with traditional female roles. Malka also had devotees of her own in the court of Belz, probably for counseling and healing. We do not know if her personal interviews with devotees reflected the same counseling methods that a male rebbe would use, as described by Rabbi

# Chapter 9

Zalman Schachter-Shalomi in his book *Spiritual Intimacy: A Study of Counseling in Hasidism* (Jason Aronson, 1986). Malka was definitely more than her husband's helpmate. Numerous stories celebrate her role in the career of her husband, Shalom Rokeach, who became the first great Rabbi of Belz. She brought the young Shalom, who was her cousin and lived in her home, to Chasidism, helping shape his future and serving alongside him as advisor in many situations. She became his eyes in old age when he lost his vision and remained the Belzer Rebbe's support until the very end of her life. Their daughter, known as Eydel of Brody, took on the functions of rebbe—some say because her husband did not enjoy that role, but other sources attribute this to her own will. While it is not clear how long she served, she did make decisions and distributed *shrayim* (food she had blessed). Her father, Shalom Rokeach, said of her, "Iss felt ir nor a spudik" (she lacks only the fur-lined hat of the rebbe). However, the Belz dynasty, which Eydel may have felt she deserved to inherit, went to the youngest son of Malka and Shalom Rokeach, instead of to the eldest son, as was customary.

While all these holy women had an important place in early Chasidic history as carriers of Shekhinah energy, they were not able to open the way for their sisters because they were perceived as "exceptions to the rule."

The one Chasidic woman whose life truly represents the emergence of the female path within Judaism was the "Maid of Ludomir," called Betulah (maiden), a nineteenth-century mystic who did not come from an established rabbinical family. She was born Hannah Rachel Werbemacher in 1805 in Ludomir, Poland. Her birth was considered the result of a blessing from the saintly Chernobyler Rebbe, as her parents had been unable to conceive prior to their pilgrimage to the saint. Considered an *ilui* or child prodigy, she was reputedly luminous from childhood like Moses, and the Shekhinah energy radiated from her face and head. At the *cheder* (religious school), she is said to have studied while sitting behind a screen. Later, as rebbe at her own synagogue (die Grüne Schule), she received visitors from behind a door and covered her face with a veil when she preached Torah. This may have

# Early Chasidism

been to protect her from outside energies or to shield others from her radiance. Traditional writers say it was to keep men from looking at her. Other examples of women using this technique include Bat ha Levi of twelfth-century Baghdad, the daughter of the Gaon Shmuel ben Eli. She is described as teaching her father's yeshiva students from behind a window.

Hannah Rachel took on the traditional male mitzvot after what may have been a near-death experience while praying at her mother's grave as a teenager. Legend has it that she fell into an empty grave, where she went into coma or altered state for a number of days. After that experience, she donned *tallit* and *tefillin* (prayer shawl and phylacteries), announcing that she had been given a new soul by the heavenly court. Her father supported her studies, and after he died, her inheritance, plus some support from local devotees, enabled her to build her own synagogue and study hall. While still a young woman, Hannah Rachel's reputation as a scholar, miracle worker, and saint grew, and she began to draw the wrath of the established Rabbinate. Ultimately a powerful beit din (rabbinical court) of three was sent to judge her. They were unable to convince her that it was inappropriate for a woman to take on the rabbinical role. (If only we had her arguments handy, they could have saved us a lot of time in the twentieth century!) She was persuaded by the influential Rabbi Mordecai of Chernobyl (a direct descendant of her parents' tsaddik) that it was her religious responsibility to marry. While complying outwardly, she refused to consummate the marriage, and the incident seems to have been part of her loss of status.

Hannah Rachel later emigrated to Israel in the mid 1850s, where she continued her kabbalistic studies and prayer until her death in 1894. The stories about her life in the Holy Land say that people followed her to the Wailing Wall; they do not indicate the gender of the Jerusalemites who sought to pray with her. She also led pilgrimages on foot to Rachel's Tomb on Rosh Chodesh. It is probable that the New Moon groups consisted of women who prayed for children at the matriarch's burial site. It became a custom for women to wear a piece of red cotton string or woolen yarn from the holy

111

site around the wrist. Folklore associated the string with protection and good fortune. (The red string made popular by The Kabbalah Centre is part of that tradition.) Clearly, Hannah Rachel continued to be a conduit for the Shekhinah's energy who led many people to the Divine Presence through her life of prayer, study, teaching, and healing.

While the Ludomir Rebbe has been written about more extensively than other women, there was a tendency for traditional authors to attack her and consider her actions as not befitting a woman. The twentieth-century research and books about her life have expanded our understanding of her importance. With the rediscovery of her burial site on the Mount of Olives just a few years ago, there has been renewed interest in her legacy. In her time, eastern European attitudes about gender were resistant to change, and the Chasidic movement had become more establishment, perhaps in response to earlier attacks by mainstream rabbis.

Eastern European Chasidism gave birth to a great variety of saints, male and female, with hundreds and later thousands of devotees. For a short historical period, Judaism assumed a spiritual-religious subculture whose mood and sensibility were more like that of India or Tibet in their discovery and cultivation of child wonders, healers of both genders, and people making pilgrimages to their magical mystical rebbes in small hamlets and larger towns. While it may have been inevitable that the conventional rabbis of the day would feel threatened, the more important question to be asked retrospectively is how this ecstatic movement came about. Was it the devotional nature of the masses at that time and their continued longing for a Messianic era, or something in the genes, some special opening in the universe? While the Chasidic revolution could not educate women overnight or bring them into synagogue life more fully, it opened the gates to the recognition of women as living carriers of the Shekhinah energy. That attitude would be carried over and resurrected in the twentieth century with far-reaching results, including the emergence of Jewish feminism and the birth of the Jewish Renewal movement with its neo-Chasidic roots.

# Meditation
## Synchronicity of Souls

You are with a group of women healers and midwives in eastern Europe who go out into the woods together to find medicinal herbs. It is autumn, and the woods are alive with the gold and crimson of the turning leaves. This group likes to share remedies for helping women in labor and sick children. They also gather to wash clothes together at the river in the warm weather; in the winter they meet at a house with a large cook stove for heating water. Although you are younger than most of the women in the group, they have recognized your spiritual qualities and have begun training you in the use of healing herbs.

The Jewish women in this town also cook together for communal events like weddings, baby namings, and holidays. Under the leadership of their *rebbetzin* (the rabbi's wife), herself a sacred teacher, they chant from the Psalms while they are cooking, infusing the food with the Holy Spirit and blessing it with the prayers that are part of their women's tradition. They have many tekhinot to cover just about any occasion. Their lives are blessed because they support and assist each other, sharing the joys and sorrows of family life.

The early fall holiday of Sukkot, the Feast of Booths, is almost over. At the end of the cycle, the community will celebrate Simchat Torah, the Rejoicing in the Law. This year it has been warm during the days of sitting outdoors in the *sukkot*, the makeshift booths. As always, this has been a time of much work for the women, carrying the food to the booths and feeding many visitors. But the prayers have been uplifting, with lots of singing and dancing. The leaders will soon commence the cycle of prayers for winter rain, and the whole Jewish community is in good spirits.

# Chapter 9

This little town is blessed with the presence of a rabbi who is a true holy man, a tsaddik. He is reputed to be a miracle worker and healer, even though his synagogue is a simple wooden building. If you look closely at the doors and rafters, however, you can see wonderful carvings of playful birds and animals by local artisans. What is special about this rabbi is that he encourages the women to kiss the Torah mantle on Shabbat and holidays, teaching that there is no prohibition on women encountering the holy scroll. With his leadership, it has become the community custom, or *minhag*, that once a year on Simchat Torah, the women are invited to take one of the Torahs into their circle and dance among themselves.

You take time to prepare yourself for these last days of the holiday. You put on your best dress and a gold necklace that your saintly grandmother left you. Since you are still single, you do not yet have to cover your long hair. While your parents will have to approve the young man who will become your husband, they want you to be a part of the process of choosing your betrothed. They appreciate your luminous qualities and want to feel sure that the one who is destined will show himself at the right time. The rabbi has intimated that such a suitor might turn up at the holiday celebration when there are many out-of-town visitors. You love this holy man who tells beautiful stories to explain the words of the Torah and the Talmud. He is very kind, receptive to everyone, and inspirational in his ability to heal all kinds of ailments. You envy the boys and men who get to spend so much time with the tsaddik in study and prayer, while the women are busy taking care of their needs.

That is why you are excited about Simchat Torah and the chance to hold the Torah. During the service, the men look so proud when they walk with the Torah procession and pronounce the blessings before the readings from the scroll. Hardly anyone knows that you know how to read from the Torah scroll and have been practicing the intonation of the blessings when you are alone. Since you were a little girl, you have been watching your father and the other men as they are carried away with singing and dancing during the prayers. You already experience devotion to God and yearn for the opportunity to enter the state of bliss that seems connected with holding the Torah and dancing.

You enter the crowded synagogue, which is decorated with green tree branches and flowers. There is barely room to move, and when the main service is over, you proceed to a special area prepared for the women in a temporary building set up in the back yard of the synagogue. There the women will continue with their own prayers and Torah circuits, known as *hakafot*. The music and dancing begin; the older women know the melodies well, and they lead the others. Soon the Torah starts circulating to the young matrons, who hold it like a beloved infant. The younger women and girls begin dancing, and soon everyone is caught up in the joy of movement. Suddenly you find the small scroll in your arms, wrapped in purple velvet. As you twirl with the Torah, you are transported to another realm where you can fly. Higher and higher, lighter and lighter, you are transformed into the sparks of light you have heard about, like liquid of many colors in the Tree of Life, spiraling up and down. The Hebrew letters are flying through the air with you and around you, and you understand the words of the prayers and the Psalms in a whole new way.

All the people are one with you, and you are one with Shekhinah. You feel the current running through you, as if every cell in your body is part of the Ruach ha Kodesh. You are connected with all these souls around you, and with the Oversoul of the world. You also have within you the simple code for ascending to this level. You hear the voice of the Shekhinah telling you that anytime you intone the Sh'ma, the prayer observant Jews repeat in every prayer service, you can propel yourself into this level of prayer and ecstasy. You are still joined with the voices of the angels, you are chanting "Sh'ma Yisrael Adonai Eloheynu Adonai Echad" (Listen Israel, the Eternal is our God, God is One) and they are responding, "Baruch shem k'vod malchuto l'olam va'ed" (Blessed is the name and the Glory of God's realm forever and ever) as you descend back into your body and your place on earth.

*Take me in under your wing*
*and be a mother and sister to me*
*let your lap be a shelter for my head*
*A nest for my rejected prayers*

—Chaim Nachman Bialik

*Modest are the gifts I bring you, I know this Mother*
*Modest I know, the offerings of your daughter*
*only an outburst of song*
*on a day when the light flares ups*
*only a silent tear for your poverty.*

—Rachel Blaustein

*And if you ask me of God, my God*
*Where is God that in joy we may worship?*
*Here on Earth too God lives, not in heaven alone . . .*
*Wherever the breath of life flows, you will find God embodied*
*And God's household? All beings: the gazelle, the turtle, the shrub, the cloud*
      *pregnant with thunder . . .*
*God-in-creation is God's eternal name.*

—Saul Tchernikovsky

*And when you, O human, will return to Nature, that day your eyes will open,*
*you will stare straight into the eyes of Nature and in its mirror you will see*
*your image. You will know . . . that when you hid from Nature, you hid from*
*yourself. . . . We who have been turned away from Nature—if we desire life, we*
*must establish a new relationship with Nature.*

—A. D. Gordon

# Chapter 10

# *Haskalah*

## Back to Zion and the Land of Israel

$C$hanges on the European scene after the French Revolution in 1848 provided Jews with more access to secular education and more opportunities to work in areas from which they had formerly been excluded. Many younger people took advantage of these openings, especially those in cities. Rural residents who left their villages seeking greater freedom and a more secular lifestyle joined the urban Jews. The new era brought increased rebellion against the piety and insular community structure in the Jewish provinces, accompanied by the desire for a more normal and physically oriented life. The growing emphasis on rational thought, science, and mathematics coincided with the development of the nineteenth-century Reform movement in Germany, which rejected many of the traditional religious modes of observance. Reform also began conducting services in German to make the liturgy more understandable.

As the liberal movement grew and spread to other parts of western Europe and the United Kingdom, some of the spiritual focus was lost, especially the ideas embedded in Jewish mysticism. The superstitious nature of Jewish life in eastern Europe came to be associated with mysticism, and both were put aside. Since the mystique of the Shekhinah was part of that mindset, the Shekhinah concept was not carried over into the teaching and thinking of the new movement. When Reform came to the United States with early German immigrants, it rapidly expanded into what is now the major stream of North American Judaism. In recent years, Jews with liberal backgrounds have become more involved in traditional study. The concept of Shekhinah is also making its way into new prayer books and songs.

# Chapter 10

The Haskalah (Enlightment) was the other movement that influenced eighteenth- and nineteenth-century Jewish life. This emancipation movement encouraged the renewal of the Jewish spirit through the revival of the Hebrew language. Its leaders, many of them poets and writers, envisioned a path rooted in nature. It was connected to the early Zionist movement, which called for a return to what was then Palestine. Though fueled by secular forces, it became the new way of expressing the yearning for the Divine Presence here on earth. Although the literature of this period is different from the mystical literature of previous eras, it exhibits the longing, love, and lyrical qualities that have always been associated with Hebrew verse. One of the most beautiful Shekhinah poems of the late nineteenth century comes from Chaim Nachman Bialik (1834–1904), the prolific writer who is considered Israel's national poet. In "Hachneesaynee Tachat Knafaich" (Shelter Me Under Your Wings), Bialik perpetuates the beautiful image of Shekhinah as mother and sister, symbol of unconditional love. Clearly drawing on his Orthodox upbringing as well as Talmudic and kabbalistic studies, he was able to bring the classical view of Shekhinah into modern Hebrew poetry. In this poem, which later became a song, he reflects the understanding of Shekhinah as cosmic feminine energy and the conduit for prayers.

The remarkable quality of this era was the coalescence of the artistic, the literary, and the political. Most of the famous Haskalah writers who emigrated to Israel were educated in Europe and brought that cultural sensibility to the new land. Some returned to visit their countries of origin from Israel, despite difficulties in travel that occurred during the First World War and other problematic times. Most had strong classical literature backgrounds, and almost all wrote in languages other than Hebrew early in their careers. The experience of discrimination against Jews was a common thread in their backgrounds. The idealism that led to the first aliyah (the early movement to resettle Israel) had the quality of religious fervor, minus the trappings of traditional Judaism, which the young idealists had hoped to leave behind along with suffering, poverty, and European anti-Semitism.

The desire to return to the land and live a wholesome outdoor life could be considered a Shekhinah-oriented philosophy expressed in modern form. The emphasis on song and dance in early kibbutz life was the bridge, with the Chasidic emphasis on joy as the way of bringing Shekhinah back to earth. While there had been praise for nature, especially in the teachings of Rebbe Nachman of Bratslav (founder and leader of the Bratslav Chasidic sect) and the Baal Shem Tov, Zionism brought that aspiration into reality. The young Zionists who emigrated to Palestine/Israel lived their dream through strenuous agricultural work. Many of those who emerged as political leaders in the newly established State of Israel (Ben Gurion, Golda Meir, et al.) also grew into political maturity after years as workers in the kibbutz movement that they helped found. Although they retained their European cultural roots, reflected in their love of classical music and poetry, their daily life was that of the collective farm, imbued with agrarian socialism and Jewish ethical values.

Many female writers and artists were also prominent in the ideology and expression of the Zionist movement. The bat kol (divine female voice) had an earthly female expression in the lyrics of Rachel Blaustein (1890–1931), who emerged as one of the best-known poets of the second aliyah period. Rachel lived the agricultural life until her encounter with tuberculosis forced her out of her kibbutz. In her poems, which became popular folk songs, she expressed her love for the earth and longing for peace in the Middle East. The poems of Kadya Molowdowsky and the paintings of Anna Ticho also express this great love for the land of Israel, along with deep sensitivity to nature.

Even as the women artists and poets were celebrating the love of the land, kibbutz women were fighting for the right to work in the fields. Most of them ended up in the kitchen, laundry, and children's houses, despite their aspirations to create a new and egalitarian Israel. Mothers gave over their infants to group care in the hope of developing generations of Israelis who would not be trapped in old attitudes about gender, work, or religion.

Chapter 10

However, the founders of the emerging Zionist state gave control of religious life in areas of birth and death, marriage, and divorce to the Orthodox, some say out of the belief that such observance would fade away with
time. In a more positive framing, we might see their yielding to tradition as
a way of honoring their connection with the families they had left behind
and acknowledging their ancestors, whose land they had come to reclaim.

Rabbi Abraham Isaac Kook, the luminous first chief rabbi of Israel under the British Mandate, recognized the Shekhinah light in the *chalutzim*
(young pioneers) and worked for harmony between religious leaders and laborers. Rav Kook saw the return to nature as part of the sacred task of the Jew
in Israel, necessary to create "strong and holy flesh." In that regard, his philosophy, emerging from a lifetime of devoted Torah study, overlapped in some
ways with the belief system of the younger generation of pioneers. They too
envisioned a messianic future of social harmony, with the added components of sharing economic resources and providing equality for women.
Those idealists could scarcely imagine how their vision and the environment
would be eroded by the materialism of the late twentieth century. The pres-
sures experienced by the Jewish state in absorbing populations from all the
continents of the world, and the continuing tensions between Israelis and
Palestinians, do not help sustain a focus on environmental concerns. Rapid
economic development also threatens the landscape of the Holy Land. Nevertheless, the passion of contemporary Israelis to know the contours of their
land and their devotion to learning about it and hiking can be seen as a continuation of the Haskalah philosophy. The commitment to exploring nature
reflected in Israeli public education and popular culture continues even today as the clearest expression of that desire.

During this same period, inspiration was not limited to Israel, as Jewish women in Europe and the United States were also moving forward. In
fact, the earlier Sephardic families had already made their mark on America
during the Colonial era. We know of the educational work of Rebecca Gratz
in Philadelphia (founder of the first Hebrew schools in the United States)

and the poetry of Penina Moise in South Carolina, and there are many others. The Shekhinah energy was especially strong in the growth of Jewish women's organizations, which engaged in social welfare directed toward alleviating women's poverty. These groups also championed the need for child care and spoke out against sexual exploitation. The issue of "white slavery" after the First World War was taken on by Die Yiddishe Freunbunde, the German women's organization led by Bertha Pappenheim. She also challenged the European Rabbinate to consider the plight of thousands of *agunot* (women who could not remarry under Jewish law if their husbands had been killed or lost in action without a body being found). The range of American heroines is extraordinary, from the fiery nineteenth-century abolitionist Ernestine Rose to the organizers of the National Council of Jewish women such as Sadie American, Hannah Solomon, and Rebecca Kohut. This was the era in which the amazing Rosa Sonnenschein established *The American Jewess*, a successful magazine (a kind of Jewish *Ms. Magazine*) published in the Midwest during the late nineteenth century that promoted Zionism, women's suffrage, and holistic health (not all the Jewish women's groups supported suffrage publicly at that time). Hadassah, the dream of Henrietta Szold, was born and still works from the Diaspora to improve life in Israel, primarily through the well-equipped hospital outside Jerusalem that serves all Israelis—Christian, Jewish, and Muslim.

These late nineteenth-century organizations evolved into effective lobbying groups for labor reform and other needed social welfare legislation. Many Jewish activists were involved in the campaign for legal birth control with Margaret Sanger, and America nourished the social-work talents of Lillian Wald and many others. Both sides of the Atlantic had Jewish women in radical anarchist and socialist groups, including the famous Emma Goldman in the United States. While she rejected religious Judaism, she was known to dance at Jewish gatherings on Saturday nights!

The shift was not only in politics and social welfare, but also in the arts and literature. Sonia Turk Delauney was painting in France. In the United

Chapter 10

States, Emma Lazarus was writing poetry inspired by the plight of the eastern European Jewish immigrants to America. Her most famous lines (beginning "Give me your tired, your poor . . . ") are featured on the Statue of Liberty in New York Harbor. In England, the philanthropic work of the Montefiores in Palestine/Israel and the teachings of Lily Montagu reached out to help shape a new awareness of Jewish culture. An elaborate history of Jewish women's historical contributions entitled *The Women of Israel* (published in 1851) was compiled by Sephardic author Grace Aguilar (1816–47) in Great Britain and is still a marvelous resource.

The inroads established by these creative women continued into the twentieth century and influenced thousands who came after them. In the United States, Jewish women moved into positions of leadership in the labor movement, of which they were an integral part. Rose Schneiderman, an impoverished immigrant who started in the milliners' union and became an official of the International Ladies Garment Workers Union, served as a labor advisor to President Franklin Delano Roosevelt. In both America and Europe, women were speaking out against injustice and trying to open the gates of equality. Some paid a heavy price, like Rosa Luxemburg, who was killed in 1919 for her outspoken leadership of radical movements in eastern Europe and Germany. Others of that era included German writers Else Lasker-Schuler and Nelly Sachs, who sounded the alarm about the threat of Nazi Germany before and during the Holocaust. Both were fortunate to be rescued from Germany before the war. Sachs, who won a Nobel Prize for her poetry—"O die Schornsteine" (Oh the Chimneys) was perhaps her best-known work—lived in exile in Sweden during the Second World War, and Lasker-Schuler spent her later years in Israel. To me, they are all the voices of the Shekhinah, calling out for peace and social justice long before the gates of equality were pushed open by the late twentieth-century feminist movement.

The legacy of these lives—including the many talented thinkers who perished in the Holocaust—set the stage for mainstream Jewish women's organizations to join forces with younger groups in the 1960s and '70s and open the way for the entry of women into fuller participation in Jewish religious life. That effort had been championed in a unique manner by Rabbi Regina Jonas (1902–44). A seminary student in Berlin during the 1920s, she completed her coursework but found her professors unwilling to ordain her. (A similar story is told of Henrietta Szold, who attended the Jewish Theological Seminary on the condition that she would never seek ordination). Ordained privately in 1935 by Rabbi Max Dienemann, Jonas worked first as a chaplain and later preached in a synagogue. Arrested, deported, and sent to Theresienstadt in 1942, she was finally sent to Auschwitz, where she was killed in 1944. We are very privileged to have a complete biography of this extraordinary woman: *Fräulein Rabbiner Jonas: The Story of the First Woman Rabbi* (Jossey-Bass, 2004) by Elisa Klapheck, who worked with Jonas's papers found in Berlin long after the war.

In her rabbinic thesis Jonas wrote, "In all love and trust to our writings and their holy ordinances, it should not be forgotten that the spirit of freedom speaks from them. May it be this spirit which speaks for woman and illuminates this question. . . . Apart from prejudice and being accustomed to it, practically nothing halachically opposes the occupation of the Rabbinic office by a woman. Thus may she in this activity advance Jewish life and Jewish religiosity for future generations."

Fifty-five years later, two hundred European women rabbis, cantors, and scholars met at a conference in Berlin. The gathering, entitled Bet Devora, was organized by now-Rabbi Elisa Klapheck and dedicated to the memory of Rabbi Regina Jonas. At that historic gathering, Rabbi Sybil Sheridan said of Jonas: "We are her future. May we live up to her ideals and prove ourselves worthy of the aspirations she did not live to fulfill."

# Meditation
## Return to Zion

Picture yourself in a gracious western European city just before the twentieth century, as an educated young man from an affluent Jewish middle-class family. You have studied philosophy and history and are on the road to a promising academic career. You wear the dark formal suit typical of your era and wire-frame glasses. You have a short, well-trimmed beard and a cultured manner that reflects your familiarity with classical languages, literature, and music. Your parents are modern thinking, and although they identify as Jews—and participate in communal charities and events—they are not religiously observant.

Recently you traveled with friends to the World Jewish Convocation in Basel, Switzerland, where you heard Theodore Herzl speak about the need for a Jewish homeland. His speech reaffirmed what you had been discussing with your peers at home, a passionate group of young Zionists who feel that it is time for a return to Palestine, where you hope to create an egalitarian socialist society that is less constrained than the class-bound environment in which you live. Although the universities in your city have opened to Jews in the last thirty years, there is still widespread discrimination and a social order that keeps everyone firmly in their place.

Your parents are adamantly opposed to these ideas about Jews going to Palestine. They see the Holy Land as dangerous, rough, and undeveloped, with little opportunity for the good life. They feel that you would be giving up a good career and a bright future if you went. To them, the whole concept is impractical, and they believe it is more important to improve the status of Jews in the Diaspora. Despite their disapproval, you and a group of friends are going to sail from Turkey during your summer vacation, when the weather conditions are favorable. You hope to persuade your family that you are going on a holiday to survey the land and that you may return in the fall. Visiting representatives of the Zionist organization help you make your plans. You cash in all your savings and cajole your father into adding some funds for the expensive journey.

When the time comes to depart, you take with you a few books of poetry, some novels, and your violin and sheet music to pass the time on the voyage. Being in a group with some resources enables you to make your way to Constantinople without major problems. But when you reach Turkey, you must deal with the demanding and rough fellows who transport pilgrims like yourselves over the seas.

In a short time, most of your money is gone, as well as many of your prized possessions. However, you are fortunate to be with your good friends, who continue to debate ideas and plans no matter how challenging the situation. The dream of returning to the ancient homeland is still in everyone's imagination. And you have had the good luck to meet a spirited young woman who is also determined to help create a new society in Israel. Her company helps you overcome your homesickness and the regrets you have about leaving your family behind.

When you finally board the weather-beaten ship (which is nothing like the ocean liner you had hoped for), you are still hopeful. Once the voyage begins, the impact of strong seas, sickness among the passengers, and an impoverished diet take over as the daily challenges to survival. When you finally reach the port of Jaffa, you feel that you have journeyed to another world. And what an exotic world! Despite the confusion of this place where you are a total foreigner, a fresh local orange tastes like manna from the heavens.

Even a short pilgrimage to Jerusalem, where only a few holy sites are open to Jewish visitors, sustains the feeling of being an outsider in a totally Middle Eastern environment. By now you have shed your European clothes and shoes and are wearing lightweight clothes and sandals more suited to the warm climate. You and your friends head north toward a land parcel—which will later become your kibbutz—near Tiberias.

As you approach the glorious Sea of Galilee with its banana groves and the smell of oranges, you begin to feel at home. This landscape is not only reminiscent of the country holidays of your childhood, it feels like a place you have lived before. While you believe this to be your future, some part of you experiences it from your past. Enlivened by the power of nature, you do your physical work willingly. You enjoy watching the vegetables grow; as the artichokes blossom, you feel as if you have given birth, and being in the fruit orchards is a source of real joy. You look at the apricots as if they were jewels and taste the oranges with deep appreciation. You feel you are eating from Mother Earth herself.

Though you had no religious training, you find yourself making the blessing over the fruit and other foods. Here it is easy to thank God for the abundance of produce and to ask for divine protection for the crops. You become more comfortable with the daily Jewish prayer cycle. With a better command of Hebrew and a renewed sense of your own being, it is easier for you to participate in Shabbat and the holidays. You have also become more caring about other people and are involved with welcoming new arrivals to the kibbutz and seeing to their needs. When the work becomes overwhelming, you manage a day down at the hot springs in Tiberias near the old synagogue, where the beautiful mosaic floors are still intact. There, looking out at the blue Lake Kinneret, you experience yourself as a true pioneer and adventurer. No longer an oppressed minority person, you have become a free man, walking on the body of Shekhinah and preparing the way for what will someday, in the future, become the State of Israel.

*We are the tree of life*
*in the Garden of Shekhinah*
*Singing a song of wonder and love*
*Ki hi m'kor ha bracha [because she is the source of blessing].*

—Hanna Tiferet Siegel

*Barchu, Dear One Shekhinah, Holy Name*
*When I call on the light of my soul, I come home.*

—Lev Friedman

*Open to me, open your heart*
*let my Presence live in you*
*I am within you, all around you*
*I fill the universe*
*Open to me, open your heart*
*let my Presence live in you.*

—Aryeh Hirshfeld

*Bruchot habaot tachat kanfei ha Shekhinah*
*Bruchim habaim tachat kanfei ha Shekhinah*
*[welcome to the women and the men under the wings of Shekhinah]*
*may you be blessed beneath the wings of Shekhinah*
*be blessed with love, be blessed with peace.*

—Debbie Friedman

# Chapter 11

# Contemporary Jewish Feminism and the Return of Shekhinah

*I*f we could take flight on the wings of Shekhinah, here is what we might see. Flying over the majority of synagogues of North America, we would see women rabbis and cantors leading prayers. We would notice that they, and some women in their congregations, are wearing *tallitot* (prayer shawls) and *kippot* (skullcaps), although more likely in colors and designs that reflect the feminine. We would see women and girls standing on the *bimah* (pulpit) reading from the Torah, as part of Shabbat services or bat mitzvah ceremonies in Conservative, Reform, Reconstructionist, and Renewal congregations. We would hear women teachers of Torah, brilliant exegetes explaining the holy texts, embodying what it means to be part of the generations of sages. We would encounter female trustees on synagogue boards and serving as presidents of congregations. Refreshments for the *oneg* (socials after services) might be provided by men or families, as opposed to the all-female cooking, baking, and hospitality roles of the past. In effect, the presence of women in leadership of Jewish communal life suggests that our access to Shekhinah, formerly connected with spiritual teachings and literature, has become apparent through women and girls calling the Divine Feminine back to earth. Perhaps this trend can be regarded as an extension of the teachings of the great Chasidic master Dov Baer, the Maggid of Mezeritch, who urged his followers to pray for the return of the Shekhinah to our planet.

The area in which the changes in the role of the feminine have been very dramatic within Judaism has been the emergence of women rabbis and cantors. Their acceptance was preceded by a period of feminist activism in the United States that included Jewish women and overflowed into many areas of Jewish life. Groups that focused on the revival of the New Moon celebration and the introduction of female God language to the liturgy were on the scene even as the struggle for women's ordination was taking place. These efforts had a significant effect on congregations, who became the employers of the more than nine hundred women rabbis (and hundreds of cantors) who have been ordained in all but the Orthodox stream of Judaism. Their acceptance in less than thirty years is confirmation of Shekhinah's presence in our time. Their impact is not just about breaking down old barriers and providing new role models; it goes much broader and deeper into new styles of leadership (now shared with male peers) that are less hierarchical and more focused on personal and family issues. The women in the rabbinate have championed tolerance for diverse lifestyles and helped open the doors for lesbian and gay rabbis. And, most importantly, they have connected with the aspirations of the greater body of women participants in Judaism who are now full citizens, counted in the minyan and called to the Torah.

These renewed members of the tribe (like the female Jews-by-choice, an important and active component in American Jewish life) are motivated to learn and work hard to become increasingly knowledgeable about the tradition. They tend to have a level of devotion that is a gift to congregational life, providing new vitality that could reinvigorate and change contemporary Judaism. Many midlife women, now parents themselves, who are already involved with providing spiritual education for their children now have an expanded role they may not have anticipated. Increasingly, they are inspiring their aging parents and stimulating them to establish new spiritual connections. The phenomenon of the younger generation bringing parents back to spiritual practice may be part of the healing needed for the generation that lived through the Second World War and carries a deep awareness of the Holocaust.

# Contemporary Jewish Feminism and the Return of Shekhinah

This trend toward expanded female participation extends into modern Orthodox circles in North America, where there are more women studying and teaching and there is a proliferation of women's prayer groups, some independent, others affiliated with a synagogue. While there have always been important roles for observant women within Judaism, there is now an expansion of public roles for inspired teachers. There are also more efforts to accommodate the role of women worshippers. For example, the modern Orthodox congregation in Berkeley, California, has for some years held a special women's Simchat Torah service (fall holiday of rejoicing with the Torah). They set up an outdoor tent, separate from the men, to enable the women to dance with the Torah for the celebration that marks the end and the beginning of the annual Torah reading cycle.

If we were flying over Israel and the holy city of Jerusalem, we might encounter more women's prayer groups and meet a few extraordinary Israeli women who have received Orthodox ordination, usually in a process of study involving three learned rabbis. The few Israeli women who already have that distinction do not serve as pulpit rabbis. While some of these new rabbis have chosen to serve as teachers rather than assume pulpit positions, there are already experiments in the Orthodox world in bridging the legal restraints on men and women sharing in communal prayer. The announcement on January 10, 2008, by the prestigious Hartman Institute in Jerusalem that it would begin a four-year rabbinical program, open to women and men trained to serve in all the streams of Judaism, including Orthodoxy, is a significant innovation. This important shift confirms the faith of Orthodox scholars like Blu Greenberg, who has predicted for many years that it would become acceptable for women to receive Orthodox ordination.

Efforts to bridge the gap have preceded this move. For example, at one modern Orthodox synagogue in Jerusalem, women pray separately from men on special occasions like bat mitzvah (providing this rite of passage for girls is not customary in most Orthodox settings). The female group assembles in a downstairs hall for the ritual and prayers and then reunites

Chapter 11

with the male worshippers for the reading of the Torah and end of the service. At a newer Orthodox congregation, also in Jerusalem, where many of the women are distinguished scholars, the minhag (custom) has been to allow women to lead certain sections of the prayers that are not prohibited under Halakhah (religious law). Men and women are still divided by a *mechitsa* (barrier), but the singing is animated on both sides of the aisle.

While these changes have taken place within synagogue life, the comfort zone for many individuals of Jewish background lies in less-structured ways of expressing spirituality. With the growth of Renewal Judaism, sparked by the leadership of Rabbi Zalman Schachter-Shalomi since the 1970s, more groups—affiliated with the Aleph Alliance—facilitate the expression of spiritual devotion and Shekhinah consciousness in joyous prayer with music and dance. Teachers in the Renewal movement, which focuses on meditation as well as prayer, incorporate traditional Torah study and immersion in Chasidic and kabbalistic teachings. While Renewal is present in Israel and Europe, it tends to be strongest in the United States. That is also true of the Chavurah movement, which pioneered more sociable and informal gatherings, some in congregations, others freestanding. The Jewish Ecology movement is likewise growing, and many young people find their spiritual parachute in Jewish camps and outdoor-oriented experiences. In fact, in recent years, all the streams of Judaism have increased their programming for families and individuals at retreat centers, camps, and beautiful settings in nature.

The Elat Chayyim retreat center that pioneered this approach offers workshops on its Connecticut campus that are enhanced by organic vegetarian food and creative children's programming. At the other end of the country, the Ruach Ha Aretz group creates opportunities for seekers to find their spiritual vitality through retreats that nourish body, mind, and soul. In the mid-nineties, a small group in California founded Ruach Ha Aretz, motivated by a shared vision of a Jewish environment that would combine love of nature with a focus on inner work and study of Jewish mysticism. The connectedness that develops in a week of shared prayer, study, and community life provides unique spiritual bonding that has included the birth of amazing children, new relationships and marriages, and profound spiritual awakenings for both newcomers and seasoned practitioners. The many miraculous occurrences that have blessed the life of the group (now an Aleph program) reinforce the belief that such efforts emulate the connectedness of Shekhinah and constitute the wave of the future. An East Coast group that focuses on nature-based Judaism is Tel Shemesh in New York. Featuring insightful teachings on its Web site and in e-mail communications, it offers creative celebrations of the Jewish calendar cycle that convey a deep understanding of the feminine within Judaism. Holiday observances, workshops, and gatherings with Tel Shemesh focus on bringing the practice outdoors (often in New York City's Central Park), sometimes in conjunction with other groups.

The Kohenet Institute, which was designed as a training program for women who aspire to a priestess role within Judaism, is another expression of the new consciousness. While the Torah specifies some of the privileges of women connected with the hereditary priesthood, it does not provide details of their functions. There are hints in the mention of the women who sit at the opening of the ohel moed (tent of meeting), presumably providing some form of blessing, cleansing, or other officiation at the sacred site.

While Kohenet (founded by Rabbi Jill Hammer) is fairly new, it is connected with earlier work done by pioneers like Rabbis Lynn Gottlieb and Geela Rayzel Raphael. Rabbi Lynn is an inspired poet and author of one of the first Shekhinah books, entitled *She Who Dwells Within*. Rabbi Rayzel (as she is known) has written and produced a vast number of Shekhinah prayers and songs. She serves as a pulpit rabbi and is the convener of a major Jewish women's gathering held in Philadelphia. That city, which is the site of the Reconstructionist Rabbinical College and the birthplace of the national Renewal movement, is also blessed with the talent of recording artist Yofiyah, who has introduced large audiences to Shekhinah through her kabbalistic Kirtan—Hebrew chanting in Hindu repetition style. A variety of groups oriented to the Hebrew goddess combine some aspects of independently created ritual with Judaic forms. These include the Mishkan Shekhinah in the San Francisco Bay Area, which offers Shabbat and holiday observances with alternating creative women leaders. Others, like Sarah's Tent, a ceremonial group in southern California now connected with the Malibu Reconstructionist synagogue, emerged from the Torah scholarship of Savina Teubal, who researched the goddess background of the matriarchs Sarah and Hagar. That focus has also been bolstered by the emergence of women's midrashim, poetry, and other art forms that attempt to recreate the feeling of prepatriarchal Judaism. The imagined ceremonial life of the Hebrew matriarchs has also been portrayed in fiction by Anita Diamant in *The Red Tent*.

The openness to Shekhinah that is being cultivated through the outpouring of new art, music, and poetry is connected to the growing interest in the study of Kabbalah and Jewish meditation. Fueled by spiritual longing, interest in Kabbalah has expanded considerably and is attracting greater numbers. Jewish mysticism is far more available now to those without Hebrew skills with the proliferation of books in English and on numerous Web sites. Courses are offered at Kabbalah centers and in synagogues and Jewish centers around the country. Some of the new practitioners are Jews who never had the opportunity to study Kabbalah in the past. I recall vividly meeting two Iranian Jewish men years ago, who told me how they had never been able to come near the esoteric information in the past because they did not have the required Torah-study background. For them, acceptance at their local Kabbalah center was a groundbreaking event. Women who attend my Jewish mysticism lectures describe their excitement at being able to read the Zohar in English and find the source of their understanding of Shekhinah. Students in Tree of Life workshops convey their relief at finding a way of putting their spiritual experiences of the Divine Feminine into a Jewish context. In these groups—and in non-Jewish gatherings as well—the feedback indicates that people already know the qualities of Shekhinah through personal intuition and dreams but have not had the Jewish context for framing that experience of the Divine Presence. Because Judaism prohibited art forms that might emulate the Divine, Jewish visionary life has been formed more by the verbal images than pictorial art or sculpture. In that respect, we might think of Shekhinah as Judaism's way of embracing the Divine Mother through a set of ethnoparticular literary filters that have been recalibrated by the sages over the generations.

Shekhinah, in her aspect of Malkhut, has been understood in Kabbalah as the energy that connects all the beings on the planet, in effect the planetary Gaia. In her supernal aspect as Binah, the mother of the cosmos, she is the source of all the planets and stars. All the souls, all planets, all stars, and all beings are woven together in a celestial pattern of intergalactic connection established by the higher force. Scientific understanding of the diversity of life forms suggests a similar concept. While the Internet and other technological advances are modeled on that cosmic intercollective, the users are not always plugged into the underlying philosophy. All these modern developments reflect expressions of an emerging Gaia consciousness, conveyed in a tangible and varied manner. They confirm the understanding that the earth is a living, breathing organism whose inhabitants are bonded together in connections that we are just beginning to understand.

The health of the planet and all who dwell here is at stake, and perhaps that is the underlying basis of the increasing use of holistic-health modalities, including acupuncture, chiropractic, homeopathy, and herbs. These techniques and others are part of the movement toward more naturally oriented healing, and hopefully the reformation of hierarchically organized medicine.

Greater acceptance of psychotherapy and other nonmedical mental-health techniques is also a part of this trend. Greater emphasis on yoga, tai chi, and various forms of body work for health and healing also represent the growing interest in ancient and modern philosophies that convey recognition of the living nature of the planet itself, the Gaia principle. Since the first walk on the moon, our understanding of earth as a living unit has clearly been expanded, and this has led to increasing interest in recycling, consumption of organic food, and awareness of the dangers of chemicals and pesticides. Added to these now are concerns about our dependence on oil and efforts to produce more environmentally friendly automobiles. We are now dealing with the sustainability of the planet, whose resources are being rapidly destroyed by greed and exploitation, resulting in serious damage to the planet's ecological health and future existence. Modern science supports the view that degradation of the environment by pollution, drought, and other maladies is endemic and threatening all life on earth. Long before this modern era of advanced scientific knowledge, the Talmud warned that the Shekhinah cannot tolerate life on earth when there is pollution, violence, and sexual abuse. The Jewish sages taught that the role of humanity is to attract Shekhinah to this level by engaging in acts of loving kindness, prayer, and generosity. That essential ethical formula needs to be merged now with our contemporary awareness so that we can become cocreators of a planetary environment that is hospitable for all life forms.

That pattern of universal connection has actually become more discernible even as its future has become endangered. Dramatic changes in climate and the increase in ecological catastrophes, reported in the media even as they are happening, could knit us together as a mutually responsible international community. We are standing at the edge of a new era, a time of emergence for the Divine Feminine. At this precipice of enlightened awareness, a longing for spiritual intimacy is reflected in the growth of all kinds of religious and spiritual movements. Sensitive approaches to dealing with illness are expanding, along with greater understanding of the personal growth inherent in aging and approaching death. Unfortunately, we have not listened enough to those who feel accompanied by God, no matter what their condition, to make those insights part of our larger cultural life. All these challenges, including the better education of children, highlight the need for love and compassion in all our institutions, whose support has been eroded by distorted values.

Ironically, we are surrounded by violence, war, and disorder at a time when the whole world hungers for peace and tolerance. Perhaps because of these multiple crises, the embrace of the Divine Mother, who is the very source of diversity, is exactly the healing needed to restore balance on the planet. Hopefully, the movement toward a peaceful future will be grounded in love for all of creation, which is her trademark. The collective harmony we long for, which is at the core of all spiritual paths, remains elusive for all of us. The growing international emphasis on sustainability and awareness of global warming serve to focus our attention on nature and highlight the importance of the Divine Feminine in the search for healing and harmony that is grounded in the understanding that we all come from the same source. In the classic Kabbalah, all life forms emerged from the Supernal Mother Binah, who is waiting to welcome us back in joy. When we return to her in *teshuvah,* there is great celebration in all the worlds. In effect, the complex philosophy of the Zohar can be boiled down to a simple slogan:

*The Divine Mother Wants You Back.*

# A Prayer to the Shekhinah
## Alicia Ostriker

Come be our mother    we are your young ones
Come be our bride    we are your lover
Come be our dwelling    we are your inhabitants
Come be our game    we are your players
Come be our punishment    we are your sinners
Come be our ocean    we are your swimmers
Come be our victory    we are your army
Come be our laughter    we are your story

# Chapter 11

Come be our Shekhinah     we are your glory
We believe that you live
Though you delay     we believe you will certainly come

When the transformation happens as it must
When we remember
When she wakes from her long repose in us
When she wipes the nightmare
Of history from her eyes
When she returns from exile
When she utters her voice in the streets
In the opening of the gates
When she enters the modern world
When she crosses the land
Shaking her breasts and hips
With timbrels and with dances
Magnified and sanctified
Exalted and honored
Blessed and glorified
When she causes tyranny
To vanish
When she and he meet
When they behold each other face to face
When they become naked and not ashamed
On that day will our God be One
And their name One

Shekhinah bless us and keep us
Shekhinah shine your face on us
Shekhinah turn your countenance
To us and give us peace

# Part 3

---

# *Shekhinah in Our Lives*

*Before a man dies he beholds the Divine Presence, towards which the soul goes out in great yearning.*

—Zohar

*Nor does the soul actually leave him until the Shekhinah shows herself to him, and then the soul goes out in joy and love to meet the Shekhinah.*

—Zohar

*When the spirit is about to depart, the Shekhinah stands over the body, and the spirit straightaway flies off.*

—Zohar

*In the future world there is no eating or drinking nor propagation nor business nor jealousy nor hatred nor competition; but the righteous sit with their crowns on their heads, feasting on the brightness of the Divine Presence.*

—Talmud

# Chapter 12

# Birth, Death, and Reincarnation

*H*uman souls prior to their birth are thought of as being part of the unified tsror ha chaim, the "treasure house of souls" or bond of eternal life, that resides within Shekhinah. It is as if their energy at that point is one with the Divine Mother and not yet differentiated by human personality or the garment of colors that we call the body. Do these individual souls already have memory and assignments, or are those given after the being is called up for active duty on the planet? One imagines a blissful soul, swaying in delightful ecstasy with its many counterparts, having its reverie interrupted because the heavenly court has decided it is time for this particular soul to incarnate. Sometimes the call to take the in-breath of earthly birth evokes a struggle on the soul's part before it finally acquiesces. Life on earth will be a radical change from the soul's protected embryonic environment, where it grows with some memory of previous bliss-filled worlds. Jewish tradition teaches that while the embryo is in the womb, it is taught all the sacred information in the universe. Once it emerges into the world, however, an angel comes and taps it on the area above the lips, instructing it thereby to forget all the wisdom it has imbibed. Presumably life on this planet requires a certain amount of forgetfulness!

Once out of the womb, we are adventurers, wanderers, in exile from our intimate connection with the higher realms, and cut off from our direct internal physical link to our birth mothers, who serve as the stand-in for the Cosmic Mother. One can look at all life as an unconscious effort to return to that state of unified being from which we emerged. While human life is presented in the Zohar as emanating from Shekhinah, the Lower Mother in

Malkhut, the soul's ultimate teshuvah (return) is portrayed as the ultimate rerouting back to the Supernal Mother, in the Upper Sephira of Binah. From that perspective, death can be seen as a goal or even a reward for a job well done. Completed, we return with the out-breath to become one again with Shekhinah. In the *yizkor* (memorial prayer), we ask that God remember the soul of the departed by reuniting it with God and incorporating it into the bond of life, that same eternal grouping. In the El Malei Rachamim prayer, which is intoned at burials, we ask that the soul of the departed find its rest under the wings of the Shekhinah, along with the most pure and the most clear of souls, whose essence shines like the light of the creation. We consign the soul into the good company of saints and angelic beings to become, again, a part of the "treasure house of souls."

A soul that exits the body during an auspicious time may have a better chance of guidance from higher levels. Hence it is considered fortunate to die on Shabbat, a holiday, or New Moon, when the alignment of energies in the universe is more favorable for direct contact with Shekhinah—in other words, a good launching time, or maybe better timing for her to "catch us in her arms"! If indeed death is but a return to our original state, albeit with a few more marks on our cosmic report card, why are we so afraid to die and so distressed by the loss of others? Is it primarily the attachment we have developed to our body, our loved ones, and our lives? Or is there a deeper anxiety, perhaps the fear of not having done the job we were sent to do?

Is our time up before we feel a sense of completion with our assignments? Will we be returning to Shekhinah empty-handed, not having healed or helped the people we encountered? Did we have the children we were destined to bring forth? (The Zohar considers those who have no children doomed to return and fulfill that mission.) Did we pass on our wisdom to our grandchildren? Did we protect the earth? Did we honor our earthly fathers and mothers and take care of them? The feelings of loss, and possibly lost opportunity, are the sources of grief for most of us who remain. We are sad because in some way we are still measuring the accomplishments of the soul on a human scale.

That quality of judgment is very present in Jewish teaching generally, and in the Zohar in particular, which suggests that our role in the afterlife is very much conditioned by our actions, or lack of same, in this life. The Zohar teaches that everyone has at least a brief glimpse of Shekhinah upon exiting the world. When the soul has that vision, it is able to go out in love and joy. The time of death is seen as one in which all one's life flashes before one in review and is presented to the higher court to render an accounting for the soul in the next world. According to the Zohar (Midrash Ha Nelam), three angels come with Shekhinah to receive the soul. One angel records good deeds and misdeeds, a second is involved with the length of one's life, and the third is the angel who has been with the individual from the womb. Another source describes the three emissaries as the Angels of Love, Judgment, and Mercy.

The Zohar describes a process in which the righteous soul attaches to Shekhinah and may even enter the River of Light directly. In dramatic narrative, it portrays the unworthy soul being assigned to a long purification process. In fact, the implication is that all souls except the most enlightened go through various levels of purification before they can merge with the light.

The soul then proceeds through the various levels of purification from the lower Gan Eden (Garden of Eden) to the upper Gan Eden, passing through the River of Light (*nehar dinur*), from which it emerges completely purified. The mythic descriptions of the upper Gan Eden contain images similar to those used in referencing the Shekhinah at Mount Sinai: "They behold the rising of the pillar of fire and cloud and smoke and shining brightness." In these beautiful passages detailing the journey of the righteous soul, the Zohar describes how the soul is healed with divine rays of light and celestial music. Before entering this phase, it is clothed in resplendent garments of light fashioned from its good deeds. After these various stages (whose exact length of time is never specified), the soul finally reaches the treasure house of souls, or tsror ha chaim, to be reunited with its source. There, in its fully cleansed and resplendent state, it is ready to be considered for its next assignment, which could be in the higher realms, or as a candidate for reincarnation back to planet earth.

The virtuous, who are thought to be worthy to be "bound up in the bundle of the living, are privileged to see the Glory of the Supernal Holy King and their abode is higher than that of the holy angels" (Zohar III:182b). That concept is already found in early Israelite thinking in the First Book of Samuel, which describes King David meeting Abigail, the wife of a local chieftain, who takes care of him and his fighters despite her husband's opposition; at that time David was an outlaw, running away from the wrath of King Saul. In his encounter with Abigail, he expresses concern about the future, but his hostess, who later becomes his second wife, tells him not to worry. As she peers into the future, she tells him that his soul "shall be bound in the bond of life with the Lord thy God" (I Samuel 25:29).

Once in that storehouse, the soul awaits its next assignment. Again, no time periods are given. The Kabbalists vary in their estimates of how many lifetimes we need to receive the understanding of what our life or lives have been about—what other traditions call enlightenment. In Jewish terms, the goal is to purify our souls and fulfill all the commandments. Some teachers say we reincarnate three times; others suggest we return as many times as necessary to learn the lessons that will enable us to complete our spiritual journey back to the divine realm. The implication is that we are given the opportunity to fulfill any assignments the soul may have been given to perfect itself. Reincarnation then serves as the finishing school for the evolving soul. Additionally, the sources are unified on the notion that even very great and saintly souls may come back to the world, mainly to assist others. In this regard, the tsaddikim are like Eastern bodhisattvas.

The literature is not very clear on whether souls come back in different genders, although the diaries of some sixteenth-century Kabbalists suggest that gender may change with incarnation. There is also no clarity as to whether souls who have been Jewish always return as Jews. Additionally, there is no unified thinking about people coming back as animals, though there have been rabbinical teachers who presented that outcome as a form of punishment.

Numerous stories about the great rabbinical figures focus on their acceptance of death and their precognition of their own deaths and the passing of others. Many of them died very consciously and peacefully, often on Shabbat or holidays and during prayer. Their way of dying seems like the ultimate reflection of faith and corroboration of their own teachings, and of the wisdom of the tradition, embodied in statements from *Pirke Avot* (Saying of the Fathers), "This world is like a vestibule before the World to Come" and "Earth is the gateway between the two worlds, the door into the heavenly spheres." A Chasidic story attributed to Rabbi Simcha Bunim of Psychka expresses the same philosophy about our priorities: "People celebrate when someone is born and cry when someone dies. It should be the reverse," he teaches us. "As they are coming in to a world of travail, we ought to weep for their lives." On the other hand, we should rejoice when they leave the world, because they have obtained the opportunity for eternal being.

The Torah actually provides the scenario for peaceful or conscious dying. Its description of Moses's death in Deuteronomy 34:5 states that Moses dies "at the command of the Lord." Traditional commentators have explicated this phrase as "by the mouth of the Lord," giving rise to the tradition that Moses died by a divine kiss. Dying by the "kiss of the Shekhinah" is ascribed to Moses, Aaron, and Miriam, as well as to the patriarchs Abraham, Isaac, and Jacob. According to the legends, Moses dies on Mount Nebo with the kiss of the Shekhinah, who carries him on her divine wings to an unknown burial site. Aaron, the high priest, like his younger brother, Moses, also dies by the divine kiss after Moses has taken him to his resting place on Mount Hor and divested him of his priestly garments (Num. 20:29). Upon Aaron's death, the clouds of glory that had shielded the people in the desert depart; other legends say the cloud comes down and covers him. Miriam the prophetess, whose death at Kadesh is noted in Numbers 20:1, is likewise presumed by the Talmudic sages (Bava Batra 17a) to have been blessed with mystical union at her death. With her death the waters dry up, since her goodness was considered the origin of the magical well that traveled with the Israelites in the desert for forty years. About these three great beings, Rabbi Menachem Recanati (1223–90) proclaimed, "Out of great devekut [attachment to God] their souls cleaved to the sublime soul [Shekhinah] until they died by a kiss."

While most of us would not compare ourselves to these great leaders of the Exodus, the implication of the mystical texts is that all beings have potential for this blissful merger with Shekhinah. Those who have led a saintly life may be better prepared to enter the ecstatic state without fear. The Zohar speaks of a proclamation going out thirty days before a person's death, describing a process in which the soul journeys to the higher realms during that time to become prepared for the passage. Those who work with the dying report the experience of feeling the Shekhinah or light energy around people who are close to death. It is almost as if the individual has surrendered the body and the ego, and is getting ready to enter another dimension. Simcha Paul Raphael (author of *Jewish Views of the Afterlife*) regards this as a kind of "nearing death" process. The transition is well stated in the words of the thirteenth-century Italian Kabbalist Rabbi Menahem Recanati, "Know that just as the ripe fruit falls from the tree, no longer needing its connection [to the tree], so is the link between the soul and the body. For when the soul has attained whatever it is able to attain, and cleaved to the supernal soul, it removes its raiment of dust, severs [itself] from its place, and cleaves to the Shekhinah; and this is the meaning of death by the kiss."

# El Malei Rachamim
## (Traditional Jewish Memorial Prayer)*

El Malei Rachamim Shokehn ba m'romim
ha m'stey menuchah nekhonah tachat kanfei ha Shekhinah
b'maalot kedoshim u'tehorim k'zohar ha rakia
mahzhirim l'nishmot yakeereynu u' k' dosheynu she halkhu l'olamom.
anah baal ha rachamim hasteereym b'steyl k'nafekha l' olamim
u'st'ror bi st'ror ha chaim et nishmatam
Adonai hu nachalatam, v' yanuchu b'shalom al mishkhavam,
v'nomar amen.

God filled with compassion, who dwells on high
grant perfect rest beneath the wings of Shekhinah
amid the ranks of the holy and the pure
who shine like the brilliance of the skies
to the souls of our beloveds and our special ones
who went to their eternal place of rest.
May you who are the source of mercy
shelter them beneath your wings eternally
and bind their souls in the treasure house of souls.
God is their inheritance and may they rest in peace.
And let us say, Amen.

*Hebrew prayer from Yizkor (memorial service) Kol Haneshamah, *Reconstructionist Prayer Book*. This version is on behalf of groups; the prayer for individuals inserts a pledge to give charity in their name. Yizkor is found in traditional prayer books for Sabbath and holidays. The translation is by the author.

*Rabbi Akiva expounded: Man and woman: if they are worthy, Shekhinah abides between them; if not fire consumes them.*

—Talmud

*When sexual relations are properly conducted the Divine Presence stands between man and wife much as it did in the Temple when the cherubim were "intertwined with one another."*

—Talmud

*When union is for the sake of heaven, there is nothing holier and purer that this union of the righteous.*

—Nachmanides

*Where there is no union of male and female, men are not worthy to behold the divine presence.*

—Zohar

# Chapter 13

# *Love and Sexuality*

$\mathcal{T}$he Talmud tells us that the Holy Temple in Jerusalem was "lined with love" by the presence of the Shekhinah—in other words, that love is synonymous with the Divine Presence, or one of her major attributes. Hidden, perhaps, but implicit is the belief that the Divine Feminine is associated with lovemaking and pleasure, similar to the qualities of the ancient Middle Eastern goddesses. Rabbi Akiva, the great sage of the second century C.E., taught that when a couple makes love that is grounded in deep spiritual connection, the Shekhinah rests between them. In this context, sexuality becomes like other mitzvot (good deeds)—such as giving charity, providing hospitality, or engaging in study and prayer—and constitutes an important way of drawing the Divine Presence to the planet. It was also Rabbi Akiva who pronounced the Song of Songs the most sacred of literature when the erotic discourse was being considered for canonization.

Commentaries on the birth of Moses say that the Shekhinah was present in the bed of his parents, Yocheved and Amram, during the lovemaking that created the prophet. According to the legends, his mother, Yocheved, had no labor pains in delivering him. The midrashim say he was born luminous, surrounded by the light of the Shekhinah, and that this light later cured his adoptive mother, the Egyptian princess Bat-Ya, of a skin ailment. Moses's relationship with Shekhinah continues into adulthood, where it becomes like that of lover to beloved. In this respect, his relationship to Shekhinah might be compared to an earlier model in which the young male consort is devoted to the Mother Goddess. He is always available to her so that revelation can pour through him daily. To be always permeable to the Divine Presence, Moses stops sleeping with his wife, Tziporah, during the later years of their marriage, after the revelation at the burning bush, when they already had their two sons. The presumed conflict with his siblings, Miriam and Aaron (recorded in the Torah in Numbers 12:1–16) is, according to midrashic sources, really about whether one can be available to Shekhinah's communication if one has an active sex life with one's partner. According to one legend, God comes to Miriam and Aaron in their beds to show them that they must purify with water after the sexual act in order to receive the Shekhinah. This seems like the other side of the coin, or a second stream of Jewish thought—that sexual fluids (like other body excretions) must be washed away before one can enter into prayer or other communion with the divine. Hundreds of years of post-Talmudic literature focused on the polluting nature of male ejaculation and the attribution of profound sin to masturbation and other forms of "wasting seed" (all presumably derived from the sin of Onan in the Torah).

The first, and perhaps most basic, line of thinking was to acknowledge Shekhinah's presence in our lives as the source of our capacity to love. This led to the idea that lovemaking could have the same quality as other actions that draw the Divine Presence near. The Jewish sages consistently counseled their male followers to imbue their romantic situations with loving kindness, concern, and gentleness. The second line of thinking seems to be that of regarding the sexual act as separate from the divine. Both philosophies, which are also reflected in the writings of the great Greek philosophers, continued to play a role in the reflections of Jewish writers on this subject. The two great medieval thinkers Maimonides and Nachmanides differed sharply in this regard, the former considering sexuality debasing, whereas the latter emphasized that all physicality was from God.

All through Jewish literary history, the sages dealt with the issue of human love and love of the Divine. Human love and sexuality were understood as earthly expressions that could never be equal to the love of God, but could emulate it. The sages considered sexuality within marriage as the proper way of bringing sacred marriage to the human level. In the early commentaries, God was portrayed as the giver (male) and the people of Israel as the receiver (female), with the Torah serving as the *ketubah* (marriage contract) between them. The metaphor for marital love was also grounded in the connection between the two golden cherubs that rested on top of the Ark of the Covenant in the Holy of Holies, where the Shekhinah descended to earth to converse with Moses. Some historians describe the cherubs as male and a female locked in a sexual embrace, who faced each other during harmonious times and turned away from each other during disturbing times, like a couple in bed. (Other commentaries say both were male, or nonhuman, perhaps angels or animals.)

While these initial concepts for sacralized marriage were based on the exalted notion of emulating the Divine, the actualization of such ideals when most marriages were arranged was unlikely. Conflict and incompatibility between marriage partners posed many challenges, which rabbinical authorities were often called upon to resolve over the centuries. Sexuality within the boundaries of Jewish marital law was always seen as a component of good family life, and the nature of a married couple's sexual behavior was a private matter. Sexual satisfaction for the woman was considered in the Talmud as one of the wife's basic rights in a marriage, along with clothing and food. In fact, she could be granted a divorce if her husband failed to perform. Some sources praise the woman who makes overtures to her husband, as the good Israelite women did in Egypt to guarantee the birth of the Exodus generation, and consider the husband responsible for responding and satisfying her. Other writers focus on the male making the overtures and setting the stage to insure a spiritual context for the sexual act. Since the man was presumably more educated and had more power in the relationship, he was expected to lead the way in providing a loving, safe atmosphere in which the woman would be responsive to his lovemaking. It was forbidden to have sex without the wife's assent, and such action was regarded as marital rape. From the Talmud on, the Judaic attitude could be characterized as consistently encouraging the expression of sexual passion and love, but only within the confines of Jewish marriage. In fact, that commitment was supposed to ensure that the husband would not be attracted to other

women. The modesty of the wife (covering her hair and dressing appropriately) and the "family purity" laws (prohibiting sex during menstruation and
for some days or even a full week after) was supposed to reinforce desire,
fertility, and legitimate offspring. Those laws, which are still part of Orthodox Jewish life, constituted the religious framework for sexual behavior in
Jewish communities at least until the mid-nineteenth century, although urban Jews had probably already deviated from the practice by then. The written opinions of the great rabbis on this subject indicate that there were always challenges to the religious laws, and that prevailing social mores in the
cultures the exiled Jews lived in also played a role in shaping the diversity of
Jewish attitudes toward sexuality over the centuries. There are fourteenth-
century Spanish documents, for example, criticizing Jewish men for keeping concubines. Although polygamy was outlawed in the tenth century, permission for concubines had a place in Jewish history. In general, men had
considerably more freedom than women in establishing relationships outside the marriage.

Medieval Jewish thinking reflects the notion that the female orgasm
was essential to the formation of the male embryo. It is not clear if that concept was older or originated in that period. If men wanted male heirs, they
had to make sure their wives were satisfied. This amazing concept—which
some scholars attribute to the wiles of the early sages intent on persuading
impulsive men to behave well—underlies some of the wonderful advice given
in a medieval Jewish sex manual entitled *Igeret Ha Kodesh* (The Holy Letter). This delightful book—sometimes attributed to the Spanish scholar
Nachmanides—was published anonymously as a sage's letter to his disciple.
It includes some highly quotable passages on the holiness of the body, and
it gives very specific advice on setting the tone before sexual relations, as
the mystical writers of that time were generally convinced that the intention of the couple during the sexual act influenced the temperament of the
child conceived during that union. *The Igeret* deals with such practical matters as which way the bed should be facing for the purpose of ensuring male

offspring. What is missing from this extraordinary treatise—and from the literature generally—is a specific prayer to be intoned before making love. The *Igeret* recommends that the husband share words of Torah with his wife and draw her into a state of holy communion but gives no specifics on language. We might well imagine the Song of Songs as a popular choice, especially on Friday night, when celebrating Israel's relationship to God in the context of the erotic sacred literature is traditional. In fact, scholars who were allowed to be away from home for their studies during the week were specifically enjoined to give their wives joy on the Sabbath.

The Zohar elaborated on the theme of the sacred marriage through the system of Sephirot, which brought Shekhinah back to Jewish thought as the Divine Mother, Divine Bride, and illuminator of women. As Matrona and Shabbos Queen, she awaits reunification with her divine lover. We on earth make that union possible through our celebration of the Shabbat. If there is a Jewish tantra, it is indeed the Shabbat, with its emphasis on candlelight, music, flowers, poetry, good food, and making love. The romantic mood is supported by ceasing ordinary activities and concerns. Shekhinah as the Shabbat opens the gateway to divine reunion, whether the coming together is same-sex or between the sexes, or the realignment of polarities with the self. It is also the time for the reconnection of the Upper Mother in Binah with the Lower Mother in Malkhut (a useful concept if one is looking for a kabbalistic basis for same-sex union). Drawing on the mystical tradition, observant Jews used the philosophy of the Zohar as the basis for encouraging sexuality on Friday night and Saturday, so that the human encounter could emulate the sacred marriage between Shekhinah in Malkhut and the Kadosh Baruch Hu (the Holy Blessed One embodied in the masculine Sephira of Tiferet). When they come together, through righteous actions and lovemaking, the cosmos is once again whole and healed. This is a wondrous and beautiful rationale for a married couple to enjoy a Sabbath blessed with spiritualized lovemaking and constitutes what could be the basis for a great sex life within marriage.

# Chapter 13

Over the centuries, what seems to have started off as the sublime idea of two people loving and satisfying each other seemed to turn into a system of controlling sexuality, and particularly of controlling the lives of women. Although Orthodox practitioners would maintain that *taharat ha mishpacha* (family purity requiring mikveh immersion after menstruation, and having sex only during the fertile time of the month) encourages passion and monogamy, for most people it is too confining, and the resulting fertility not what all couples are seeking. When Jewish marriages were arranged, there were many unhappy couples. Lack of sexual education in previous eras and prohibition of premarital sex resulted in marriages that were far less than ideal. While Judaism accepted sexuality for personal fulfillment and not just procreation, the rules developed by all-male rabbinical authorities lacked input from women and from those less observant. As a result, there were always those who broke from the system.

The early leaders of the Haskalah movement criticized the narrowness of Jewish religious life regarding sexuality and called for a more open and natural approach to relationships between the sexes. That attitude informed the early period of the kibbutz movement in Israel and spread to the growing secular Israeli population, which rejects the authority of the rabbinate over its sexual life. Ironically, Israelis are still dependent on that same authority for legitimization of marriage, circumcision, and divorce.

Although liberal and conservative rabbis perform life-cycle rituals in Israel, their ceremonies are not recognized by the ultra-Orthodox establishment, and civil divorce does not exist in the Jewish state. While divorce was always possible under Jewish law, it relied on the willingness of the husband. That and other aspects of the old laws worked against women.

In recent years, the Torah's teaching on homosexuality has become a divisive issue among Jewish denominations. Most modern liberal Jewish movements have moved into full acceptance of gays and lesbians within Jewish life, and their ordination as rabbis has proved to be a significant dividing line between the Orthodox and others, just as have the issues of abortion,

Love and Sexuality

birth control, and the ordination of women. The acceptance of homosexuality among most American Jews has stimulated significant examination of the biblical injunctions, especially within the Conservative movement. We might say that the liberal wings of Judaism in the United States look to the tradition for inspiration and wisdom, while retaining their freedom to set aside laws that reflect a narrowness of viewpoint grounded in earlier historical periods.

On the other hand, the sexual codes in the Torah, which we read on Yom Kippur, still seem relevant to the modern era when they speak of prohibition of incest and relations with close relatives. The Talmud is very specific in its statement that the Shekhinah cannot tolerate rape or incest. Rabbi Akiva taught that when sex is purely physical or does not emerge from love, the Shekhinah's presence turns to fire; that heat, expressed as lust, or sex with violence, becomes the destroyer. Certainly our modern experience concerning sexual abuse continues to affirm this view.

*If one dreams that he is reciting the Sh'ma, he is worthy that the Divine presence should rest upon him.*

—Talmud

*A person should remember a good dream, so that it will not be forgotten, then it will be fulfilled.*

—Zohar

*A man is shown in a dream only what is suggested in his own thoughts.*

—Talmud

*When a man is asleep at night, his soul goes and testifies to all that he has done during the day.*

—Zohar

# Chapter 14

# *Divine Guidance in Dreams*

*J*ewish thinking presents dreams as messages from the Divine—signals to enable us to understand ourselves better and to realign our lives with the divine plan. In that respect, dreams represent an intimate and direct personal communication between the individual and the Ruach ha Kodesh, similar to the gift of prophecy and vision. Because dreams are conveyed through the mechanism of the personal imagination, we can regard them as an inside line to Shekhinah. Mother and educator, she uses our unconscious to alert us to feelings and situations that we are less likely to access in our busy waking state. Talmudic teaching regards all dreams as one-sixtieth of prophecy. True *neviuth*, or prophetic vision, was considered to flow from the direct connection with Shekhinah on the part of the prophet, and the tradition has special respect for the dreams and visions of the patriarchs and prophets. For those enlightened individuals, there was little differentiation in the Torah among dreams, visions, and prophecy. The Torah details the interpretations of Joseph, who rose to a high position in Egypt following his premonitory understanding of Pharaoh's dreams. In ancient cultures, the dreams of the kings were very highly valued. A similar pattern is apparent in the life of the prophet Daniel, who was captured as a youth by the Babylonians in their conquest of Israel. His ability to interpret dreams was recognized, and he became a protected member of the court of King Nebuchadnezzar. Like Joseph, he also dealt with the future of the Babylonian empire based on the king's dreams. The Jewish sages believed the prophet's dreams represented direct communication from the Divine because the prophet, who prayed and fasted to enhance an already special awareness, had greater potential for the Divine Presence to rest on him or her. Such a prophet also had the ability to be the channel for the group dream—the vision that spoke to the condition of the nation, or, indeed, all of humanity.

The Hebrew regard for the dreams of the patriarchs and prophets has its parallel in the surrounding cultures, which also believed that the dreams of their leaders emanated from the Divine Source. The various Middle Eastern cultures with which the Israelites had contact over an extended period all utilized specialists in oracular and magical practices, some of which were oriented to the interpretation of dreams. While the Torah warned repeatedly against engaging in any of these forms—and detailed the unacceptable ones, such as necromancy—the Israelites had their sacred oracle, known as the Urim U' Tummim (Lights and Perfections), which were consulted by the high priest for the sake of the nation's health. The device consisted of a metal breastplate with twelve gemstones representing the twelve tribes, which lit up in a manner that the high priest could interpret. At the time of the First Temple in Jerusalem, the high priest would make an inquiry and was trained to decipher the response in the form of certain areas being illuminated. In effect, he served as the national interpreter, based on the belief that the Divine Presence rested on him. The Talmud outlines that process as follows: "We turn to the one we are consulting and they in turn face the Shekhinah on our behalf" (Rabbinical Baraita, Talmud Yoma 7:73a). This oracular system, which was not consulted after the time of King David, was lost with the destruction of the temple and was never recovered, nor was any comparable process even reinstituted for consulting the Divine on behalf of the Jewish people. This is also true for the area under the ark known as the Mercy Seat (supposedly where Moses is said to have had direct contact with the Shekhinah). That area continued to be in use when the high priest, entering the Holy of Holies, also communicated with the Divine Presence. After the destruction of the First Temple, these methods of asking for revelation were no longer viable or were simply lost. While the Babylonian Jews had their prophets and visionaries, they no longer had the pomp and circumstance of the temple rituals to sustain the collective vision. However, they were living in a culture that honored dreams and that may have influenced the serious consideration of personal dreams in the Babylonian Talmud.

The Talmud contains numerous insights about the importance of the dream state and references the dreams of the great teachers, who posed questions in their dreams and sometimes tried to invoke visits from holy sages in the other worlds. In the Talmudic view, ordinary people could also be dreamers and perhaps even receive predictive information in their dreams. However, it was considered more likely that their dreams would contain more of the daily matter, and thus be a less-pure communication, or possibly one that had less significance for the community at large. The Talmud says that there is no dream without some trivia. The sages recommended that individuals seek out interpreters, and there were professional dream interpreters around the time of the redaction of the Talmud (200–400 C.E.). The Talmud cites twenty-four dream professionals in Jerusalem alone and indicates that they were paid a fee for their services or given gifts. These individuals were seen as having special intuitive skills, known as *Chokhmah* and *Binah* (wisdom and understanding), which empowered them to bring forth deeper awareness of God's intent for their clients. The interpreters probably included famous rabbis and scholars, suggesting an approved Jewish approach to the interpretation of dreams. And there appears to have been some ecumenical exchange as well. Fourth-century Jews reputedly went to Chaldeans for interpretation; pagans went to Jews, and so forth.

While the Talmudic writings and those of Philo support the idea of a period in Jewish history in which dream life was accorded an honored place, we have little written about the breakdown of that attitude. The shift in cultural perspective is probably related to the loss of country and culture that accompanied the conquests of Israel and the subsequent dispersion of the Jewish people to various countries of the Middle East and Europe. With the destruction of the Second Temple by the Romans in 70 C.E., prophecy was believed to have truly ended. Just as some sages taught that the Shekhinah could not live anywhere but in her holy abode in Jerusalem, so prophetic vision is said to have been extinguished with the loss of the temple and the land. After the Roman conquest and exile, recognition of prophetic qualities in individuals was unlikely and regarded with suspicion. Conquest led to dispersion in predominantly Christian European countries, where Jewish culture could not sustain the same unity that had characterized the shorter seventy-year Diaspora in Babylon. The Babylonian spiritual climate and culture were also more congruent with Jewish customs and lifestyle. It is likely that the importance of personal dreams diminished over time as collective Jewish life and prayer became consumed with the singular dream of returning to Zion.

Nevertheless, some medieval Jewish communities continued the romance with the personal dream world. The Yehudei Ashkenaz (pious Jews of the early medieval era) considered dreams as "windows to the soul" and placed great emphasis on righteous thoughts and actions, believing that such efforts would lead to good dreams. In the writings of Yehudah Ha Chasid, the leader of the Franco-German Pietists, there are references to the Jews of that period going to their sages for interpretation of puzzling or troubling dreams. The stories related indicate the importance ascribed to significant personal dreams. Other scholars (both Ashkenazi and Sephardi) continued using the procedure for asking dream questions. Even Maimonides, considered an Aristotelian thinker, who ascribed dreams to mental phenomena rather than communication with the Divine, wrote an extensive treatise on dreams.

The Zohar, expanding on the fascination with dreams, speaks of the soul leaving the body and traveling at night up to the halls of heaven, where it plays with God and the angels. It also refers to special birds of the night who carry people's thoughts up to the throne of glory. In this schematic, the purer one's thoughts, the more likely one is to receive an illuminating dream. Presumably, the more enlightened the dreamers, the less likely that the business of daily living will dominate their dreams. The sixteenth-century

# Divine Guidance in Dreams

Kabbalists of S'fat in northern Israel, who meditated together and individually at night, surely understood the value of dreams and probably focused on receiving visionary dreams.

We now have a translation of *Sefer Ha Chizionoth*, the dream journal of Chaim Vital (1543–1620), one of the most important members of the Lurianic circle. Many of the circle's practices—such as fasting, isolation, prayer, and journeys to holy sites—were focused on the process of receiving visions of the Shekhinah. It is likely that they enlisted the help of the archangels through special prayers, including those to the Angel Gabriel, who is considered the gatekeeper of dreams, known in Hebrew as *saar ha chalomot*.

It was around this same time (mid-sixteenth century) that the work of Rabbi Solomon Almoli emerged, entitled *Pitron Ha Chalomot* (The Interpretation of Dreams). Almoli (1490–1542) was a Sephardic scholar who emigrated to Turkey. In his book he attempted to renew Judaism's interest in dreams, including a dream dictionary along with his treatise to enable individuals to analyze their own dreams. He was convinced that individuals could have their destiny revealed through understanding their dreams. This material has been translated by Joel Kovitz in his wonderful book *Visions of the Night*, which provides us with strong insights into Almoli's thinking.

Later generations of great Chasidic rebbes popularized the importance of visionary experiences and interpreted the dreams of their devotees as a way of teaching and counseling. This renaissance of interest in dreams was connected to the personalities of the tsaddikim, who were probably lucid dreamers. Their followers would have especially valued the dreams of their teachers and chosen to emulate them. However, other European Jews moved away from the mystical beliefs of the Chasidim into a more contemporary, rationalist orientation. The avenues for leadership also changed, with some of the energy moving to the secular, political, and ultimately scientific areas in which intellect and insight could be expressed in a more contemporary fashion. While many of the great nineteenth-century rebbes were in touch with modern philosophies, the Chasidic world was increasingly perceived

as superstitious and caught in religious rigidity. Jewish rationalism put aside
amulets and prayers for healing, looking to modern medicine to deal with
health issues. Jewish secularism minimized the importance of the dream
world, relegating it to the lives of women and religious mystics, until Sigmund
Freud and Carl Jung made dreams important again. The development of
psychoanalysis and the resurgence of emphasis on dreams allowed for renewed interest in what Judaism had to contribute to the area of dreaming
and dream interpretation.

The following eight principles are the main components in the Jewish
philosophy of dreams:

- Dreaming is holy work, and retelling dreams is a high priority.
- Every dream is important and deserves serious attention and
  appropriate interpretation.
- One should share dreams with friends, but only with those one
  can completely trust.
- The knowledge, wisdom, and intuition of the dream interpreter
  is very important, since this individual is taking on a very sacred
  role.
- No matter how well trained the interpreter, he or she must always consider the situation and personality of the dreamer in
  analyzing the dream.
- All dreams are sending us messages from the Divine Presence
  so that we can improve our lives and carry out our assigned work
  in the world.
- There are positive and negative dreams. Many dreams are challenging, so that we can see where we are off and realign ourselves.
- Negative dreams can be transformed to good with appropriate
  rituals (such as fasting), charity, and prayer (see "Hatavat Chalom:
  Amelioration of a Disturbing Dream" below). Fasting the day after a challenging dream probably goes back to Talmudic times

and is reinforced in the Zohar, which states, "A fast is as good for a dream as flax for fire."

These principles are remarkably similar to the concepts of contemporary dream-work. Omitted from the list is the Jewish idea that some dreams come from demonic sources, or that they are generated by those who specialize in occult practices with negative intent toward others.

These attitudes, expressed in early Jewish writings, probably grew out of some need to differentiate Jewish dream practices from those of the Greek mystery schools, which had clear techniques for incubating dreams and consulting dream oracles at the special temples set aside specifically for those practices. Jewish practice continued to focus on the role of prayer and fasting as a way of dealing with difficult dreams. Since Hebrew was not taught to all women, we suspect that they may have dealt with their dreams differently. For the initiated, the prayers could serve as the modality for calling in the Divine Presence. For those not versed in Hebrew, the dreams remained, along with the individual prayers of the heart, as spontaneous conversations with the Beloved.

## Hatavat Chalom
### Amelioration of a Disturbing Dream

One who has a dream that causes anxiety should gather three friends, tell them the dream, and then carry out the following procedure seven times.

The dreamer says:

| English | Aramaic |
|---|---|
| I have seen a good dream | *chelma tova chazai* |
| I have seen a good dream | *chelma tova chazai* |
| I have seen a good dream | *chelma tova chazai* |

# Chapter 14

The friends respond:

| | |
|---|---|
| You have seen a good dream | *chelma tova chazeyta* |
| You have seen a good dream | *chelma tova chazeyta* |
| You have seen a good dream | *chelma tova chazeyta* |
| | |
| Your dream is good | *chelma deedach, tova hu* |
| and may it be good | *v' tova l' hevee* |
| Let the Merciful one turn it to good | *rachmanah lish'v yay l'tov* |
| | |
| May they decree on it | *sh'va zimnin yigzarun* |
| from heaven seven times | *aley min sh'mayah* |
| | |
| that it be good. | *dee y hevay tovah* |
| It is good and may it be good. | *tovah hu, v tovah l' hevee.* |

Blessed is Adonai forever, Amen and Amen.

It is the custom of some to then give the dreamer the priestly blessing (this is a modified translation of the traditional language from the *Orot Sephardic Weekday Siddur,* based on the Talmud):

> May God bless you and watch over you
> May the Divine countenance shine on you, and be gracious to you
> May the Presence of God be available to you always, and give you peace.

Another practice during the public priestly blessing (Talmud Berachot 55a):

> Whoever is in distress on account of a dream should recite during the time the priests spread forth their hands, the following:
> "O Master of the World, I am Yours and my dreams are Yours."
> For that is a propitious moment, and if one then offers up the prayer in distress, Rigour is then turned to Mercy.

*Whoever pronounces the benediction over the New Moon in its due time, welcomes, as it were, the presence of the Shekhinah.*

—Talmud

*You have given us festivals for joy and new moons for remembrance. And when we were in Jerusalem, city of beauty, the seat of the dwelling house of our Mother the Shekhinah, of all beauty, the heads of the community would consecrate* [the new moon].

—Rebbetzin Leah Horowitz

*May it be the will of God of the heavens to establish the house of our life and to return the Divine Presence to it . . . speedily in our days. Amen.*

—Traditional prayer book

*God's crescent kiss renews us again and again.*

—Susan Berrin

# Chapter 15

# New Moon

*L*ike most ancient cultures, Judaism allegorized the moon as female, probably because of the similarity of its phases to the human menstrual cycle, and the sun as male. In the commentaries on the first chapter of Genesis, the moon and sun start off as equals at the beginning of time, but the moon is diminished when she complains to God about having to share equal billing with the sun. However, she is promised a return to full size in the Messianic era, implying the eventual equality of the human male and female. She is then placated with the prospect of God requiring New Moon sacrifices and prayers when she emerges. The moon, like the people of Israel, goes into exile but always comes back. Likewise the Shekhinah, once the proud mistress of the Holy Temple in Jerusalem, is exiled and humiliated by the conquering nations. But there is always the prospect of her being redeemed and her sovereignty restored by the righteous acts of her people.

According to Jewish legends, Israelite women were "given" Rosh Chodesh (new moon) as a women's holiday because they refused at Sinai to contribute their jewelry to the construction of the golden calf. We know that moon celebrations had already existed among the indigenous Canaanite people and the neighboring cultures. In effect, Jewish law provided official sanction and an additional spiritual dimension to an already existing practice. There were probably ancient full-moon practices as well, which were retained in the Shelosh Regalim (the three pilgrimage holidays) of Passover, Shavuot, and Sukkot holidays, which always fall on the full moon, as does Purim in the early spring.

Perhaps in honoring women with the gift of Rosh Chodesh, Judaism was also acknowledging the congruence of the moon's phases with the female menstrual cycle, which features renewal and potential for new birth (crescent moon), the glory of pregnancy (full moon), and the gradual closing of the cycle represented by menopause (waning moon). Classically, these would be the maiden, the mother, and the wise-woman stages in the life of a woman. Moon goddesses abound in Middle Eastern history; and as we have seen, the early Israelites were especially aware of Asherah and Astarte, who were part of Canaanite and Ugaritic culture. According to the Torah, all the matriarchs grew up in goddess-worshipping areas and probably had knowledge of the rituals associated with those deities, since their immediate families were involved in pagan practices. Goddesses in those predominantly agricultural societies placed emphasis on prayer and worship of the female deities as part of the periodic replenishment of the earth. The moon was seen as a nurturer and was probably experienced by ancient peoples as having an effect on the growth of the crops.

At Tel Hazor in northern Israel (an ancient archeological site excavated by Yigael Yadin), there is a small figure that is considered to represent the male moon god, Sin, in the ancient Babylonian pantheon. Sin was popular at least until the third century B.C.E. He is often portrayed as traveling through space in a crescent-shaped boat with a full moon over his head. Some ethnographers think that Mount Sinai was named for him, and that the Israelites thus received the Torah on the moon mountain. In the small, detailed stone carvings found at Hazor, the figure is standing on a crescent, and his hands are upraised in a gesture of blessing to the full moon. While Jewish tradition forbids worship of sun, moon, and stars, Jewish rituals for blessing the moon recognize its importance to the human psyche. Kiddush Levanah, the traditional prayers for sanctifying the new moon, also contain elements we might easily see as pagan—jumping toward the moon and invoking prayers for protection from evil—but with added religious elements that make the ritual part of established Jewish practice. The sages caution us to honor the heavenly bodies and nature not as deities, but as important elements in God's creation.

# New Moon

During the era of the central Jewish temples, New Moon celebrations included specified sacrifices accompanied by priestly blessings and Levitical music. A unique contribution was the special ceremony for cleansing the people of their mistakes. Based on the notion of renewing self and community each month (like a woman's cycle), the priest cast blood in various directions. These ceremonies were carried out by the high priest or prince to ensure the flow of renewed energy into the community. Shekhinah's protection for the people was invoked through the temple practice for all Israelites, but no doubt most dramatically for those in the city who were able to attend the ceremony. The mood of introspection and renewal was reinforced by the custom of visiting a prophet, which often took place in provincial settings at local shrines (referred to in I Kings chapter 4 in the story of the prophet Elisha and the Shunnamite woman). The moon, like the Shekhinah, was associated with prophecy, and it was believed that on Rosh Chodesh people had a greater capacity to see into the future.

Rosh Chodesh was also the time for gathering with family and friends, reflecting belief in divinity as the source of connectedness. (In this regard, Shekhinah functions like a kind of spiritual glue that holds the universe together. *Devekut,* "attachment" or "devotion," relates to *devek,* meaning "glue.") The practice of visiting for a special meal on Rosh Chodesh—dating at least back to David being expected at the table of King Saul (as recorded in I Samuel 20:5)—was carried forward in history in the customs of Middle Eastern Jews. It was their practice to gather with the extended family on Rosh Chodesh to offer prayers and intentions for the new month. These gatherings, like Shabbat, were celebrated with ritual candle lighting and a festive meal to honor Shekhinah's presence. The underlying Jewish assumption is that Rosh Chodesh, like Shabbat and the holidays, offers a unique opening to the Shekhinah. It is as if the Divine Presence is more available at these times, serving as a divine facilitator for prayers and meditations to ascend. While Middle Eastern home rituals for the New Moon involved the whole family, there were also separate women's gatherings.

# Chapter 15

In both Eastern and Western cultures, gatherings of women guaranteed the perpetuation of moon awareness as sacred time. Women's informal ceremonies probably stayed closer to the old nature celebrations in which the Divine Mother was honored through music, dance, and food and drink. Communal worship also included bonfires in ancient times. Women's candlelighting may have become the substitute for the fire lighting in the ancient temple, just as women baking challah took the place of the temple showbread. In this vein, perhaps taharat ha mishpacha (family purity law) is the substitute for the cleansing rituals carried out by the high priest on behalf of the people. Both tracks—the female informal and the more structured male—continued throughout the Jewish Diaspora, with great rabbis offering answers to legalistic questions regarding appropriate New Moon observance and prayer.

Lurianic philosophy, developed by the sixteenth-century Kabbalists of northern Israel, amplified the understanding that the time right before Rosh Chodesh is optimal for forgiveness and the resolution of conflicts, releasing old patterns in order to be renewed by the moon. From this came the practice of Yom Kippur Katan (minor Day of Atonement) among the followers of Rabbi Isaac Luria, in which community members publicly aired the problems within their circle and asked for forgiveness from each other. One would thus prepare for the appearance of the fresh crescent by moving into the quality of forgiveness, which is associated with God's quality of patience, (*erech apaim*). The Shekhinah is portrayed, even in pre-Talmudic writings such as the *Pesichta d Rav Kahana*, as always trying to shape us up morally. Despite our backsliding, she has infinite patience, like a long-suffering mother, and calls out to us repeatedly to mend our ways before it is too late. The moon time thus became an opportunity for monthly realignment to the Divine.

Chasidic practice, which drew on this earlier period, tended to emphasize Rosh Chodesh as a time for prayer and celebration. In Israel there are great prayer gatherings on Rosh Chodesh at the Western Wall, called by leaders of the Orthodox Jewish establishment, especially during times of national crisis. Among the Ethiopian Jews there is a holiday known as Siged that falls on the new moon of the month of Kislev (usually November–December), which also focuses on asking divine intervention regarding major problems facing the entire community. Observant Jews are familiar with the announcement of the new moon in the synagogue before its appearance, and with the additional prayer (Yaaleh V Yavo) intoned on Rosh Chodesh. Those who participate are also conversant with Kiddush Levanah, the special prayers for blessing the heavenly body after her appearance in the night sky. Hundreds of years of scholarly focus on when and how to do those prayers were embedded in the *sheilot u' teshuvot* (questions and answers) of great rabbis.

As religious observance fell in contemporary society, awareness of the moon cycles as a sacred practice also declined. However, the dramatic emergence of women's New Moon groups, rituals, and books in the 1970s and '80s were a testament to the enduring attraction that the moon continues to exercise on our inner life. In an atmosphere of feminist activism, Jewish women became more outspoken and ready to reclaim the customs of their foremothers in a style that fit with modern consciousness. Additionally, celebration of New Moon was not as legalistically bound as Sabbath and Holy Day observance, making it more accessible for women. New prayers, poems, and songs emerged, written by lay people and the newly ordained women cantors and rabbis. Much of the initiating energy came from groups in Boston, energized by the leadership of Penina Adelman and her groundbreaking book *Miriam's Well,* which offered ritual processes to those wishing to start their own groups. With the integration of processes developed in the human potential movement with feminist writings and Judaic scholarship, a whole new wave of women's ritual and ceremony was born. Many of the groups were affiliated with synagogues, but others were independent. Most were all female, with some of mixed sex.

# Modern Blessing for the Sabbath before the New Moon

(Excerpt from the *Birkat Ha Chodesh* song by Cantor Linda Hirschorn.)

> And grant us many years to live
> Seeking peace and justice for the world
> Sustained by our friendships and not by wealth
> Renewed by the cycles of the moon
> A life that's filled with the love of the Torah
> A love of the Torah and the wonders of the world
> A life that fulfills the yearnings of our heart
> Renewed with the cycles of the moon.

## Sanctifying the New Moon

(Excerpt from the Kiddush Levanah by Rabbi Geela Rayzel Raphael.)

Blessed are you Shekhinah, Queen of the World.
You whispered the sky into being with the breath of Your voice.
All the celestial hosts delight and rejoice fulfilling Divine Will.
You fixed them in time and space so they will illuminate everlasting.
She is Truth Worker and Her work is Truth.

To the moon she said:
"May you renew your crown of Beauty
for those with full bellies.
They renew themselves like Her
and adorn their Creator for the sake of Her glory."

Blessed be *Rachamemah*, Source of New Light,
Renewer of the Moon in her seasons.

*"The Shekhinah hovers over the head of one who is sick." . . . Therefore, those who perform the mitzvah of* bikkur cholim *are obliged to sit low on the ground in reverence for the Divine Presence.*

—Talmud

*When we perform the mitzvah of* bikkur cholim, *we encounter the Shekhinah's presence, for the Divine Presence is there both for the person who is ill and for those who are attending to his needs.*

—Estelle Frankel

*The divine Presence does not rest on a man plunged in gloom.*

—Talmud

*Nature does not operate on its own, the Hand of God is as operative in natural events as in the supernatural. Remedies are assumed to be purely natural phenomena, as when a particular medication cures a disease. But through nature, as well as through miracles, we must see the work of God.*

—Rabbi Baruch of Medzeboz

# Chapter 16

# *Spiritual Healing*

*A*ll spiritual healing represents an opportunity to align the self with the Divine Presence. Although the Shekhinah is always available, crisis often makes the individual more willing to reach out for the light and more conscious of its presence. Healing can involve alleviating or curing a condition, or becoming more graceful in one's acceptance of its role in one's life. Sometimes both happen at the same time. In Jewish tradition, the effort on the part of the healer or the community is to call upon the divine power to assist the affected individual and their loved ones to come through the crisis. Our oldest documented example is Moses's brief but moving prayer in Exodus on behalf of his sister, Miriam the prophetess, in which he cries out, *El nah r'fa nah lah* (Please God, heal her). To this day, the most commonly used technique is prayer, or study and devotional reading of *tehillim* (the Psalms). Community prayers for healing (known as mi sheberach), which are done in the synagogue when the Torah is read—usually on Shabbat in contemporary synagogues—draw on the power of the holy scroll and the assembled energy of the community to ask for God's help. In contemporary circles, many congregations sing modern melodies written to these mi sheberach blessings or to the *El nah r'fa nah lah* prayer. The community prayers call upon the grace of the ancestors to be drawn into the healing of those we name aloud. It also serves to inform the community of serious health challenges so they can continue praying or offer practical assistance with care, food, and healing visits, referred to as *bikkur cholim*. While visiting the sick is carried out nowadays primarily by rabbis and chaplains, all Jews are encouraged to participate in that mitzvah. The practice is discussed in the Talmud, and specific recommendations for visiting the sick are detailed in the writings of Maimonides. Instructions are also contained in the compendium of religious laws known as the *Shulchan Aruch*. In effect, the sages attempted to codify elements of the healing visit. The Spanish sage Nachmanides taught that visiting the sick was incomplete if we did not also intone a prayer on the sick person's behalf. The Talmud teaches that the Shekhinah rests on those who are ill, hence the person visiting is also blessed by the Divine Presence.

In biblical times, all healing was considered to come from God, based on the Torah's description of God as healer of the sick. During temple times, the priests may have served as intermediaries to assist the individual with prayer, fasting, or atonement that might facilitate the healing process, in addition to whatever medical or herbal techniques were available. The priestly class would also receive the offerings of gratitude brought after a recovery from an accident or illness. During the centuries that followed the destruction of the First Temple, there are numerous stories of sages and prophets who brought about miraculous healings. While that is clearly part of the tradition, the redactors of the Talmud and Mishnah were wary of charismatics who might present themselves as magical healers. The criteria seem to have been whether the individual was acknowledged as learned, God fearing, and saintly. Many of the great rabbis were themselves what we might call faith healers and did some form of laying on of hands.

The Babylonian Talmud expresses support for the work of physicians, and Jewish teaching from the Talmud on regarded physicians as intermediaries, serving God, the one true healer. While there was some form of Jewish medical and herbal training prior to the Greek conquest of the Middle East in the fourth century B.C.E., the influence of Greek philosophy and medicine helped create a new medical profession and reduce suffering from the illnesses that afflicted the populations of the Middle East. Even as Jewish healers absorbed Greek teachings about the body, they probably retained the religious and cultural aspects that characterized Jewish medicine. Among the Jewish sects of the Second Temple era, in which both Greek and Roman influences were powerful, there were groups that were very much focused on spiritual healing, including the Essenes in the Dead Sea area and the Therapeutae, a semi-monastic community chronicled by Philo. The teachings and work of Rabbi Yeshua (Jesus of Nazareth) are often viewed in the context of that turbulent period. The emergence of early Christianity is intimately connected with this issue of spiritual healing. After the destruction of the Second Temple in 70 C.E., Jewish health practitioners who were exiled to Christian Europe found themselves in the position of "other," even if they were trained as doctors or midwives. Medical training in Christian countries was closed to Jews and women, probably until the early Middle Ages. However, contemporary researchers have found that midwives crossed the religious divide and tended to use similar techniques and have knowledge of herbs. Perhaps because of need and skill, many Jewish physicians ended up being recognized and utilized, sometimes by the princes and rulers of Europe. The Islamic influence in Spain during the era when scholars were literate in Arabic, Hebrew, and Latin may have facilitated greater acceptance of Jewish practitioners.

The rigorous study and focused application required for proficiency in the fields of medicine and law is often compared to the requirements for study of Talmud, perhaps accounting for the attraction of Jewish students to these professions. Jewish doctors were trained in Hebrew, master teacher to student, in a manner similar to the training of scholars. Over the centuries, many of the great Jewish sages were also physicians, and many Jewish physicians, even now, are learned and observant.

While European Jews sought out trained medical doctors, the work of midwives and herbal healers continued, probably more so in rural areas with limited medical resources. Likewise, in both Europe and the Middle East, the tradition of saintly healers continued. With the development of eastern European Chasidism, an afflicted individual might be brought to visit a saint, with a request for prayers of intervention. During the halcyon days of the great Chasidic masters and the Mizrachi teachers who were known to be miraculous healers, the individual involved might also receive a special "prescription" from the holy person or tsaddik/tsaddeket. In this situation the tsaddik, rebbe, or seer would use intuitive powers to discern the psychospiritual basis of the illness and look for healing in that realm. Long before modern psychology, Jewish healers emphasized the profound connection between the emotions and physical ailments. The Chasidic masters in particular understood the underlying mental and spiritual issues that could precipitate physical illness. The belief in the connection between the emotional and the spiritual goes back to early commentaries on the Torah, which tell us that the patriarch Jacob lost his connection with the Shekhinah during the years that he mourned for the loss of his favorite son, Joseph. Regardless of time period, the central theme of Jewish spiritual healing is that disconnection from spirit lies at the root of emotional problems. In that respect, Judaism has always taken a holistic approach to healing, regarding the body, mind, and soul as interconnected.

Many of the Chasidic and kabbalistic saints were reputed to be able to "read" the soul and its previous incarnations, known as *gilgulim*. The Ari—Rabbi Isaac Luria—is said to have read faces and hands, for example. After discerning what the person's problems were, the saint might assign specific prayer practices or create a healing amulet for the patient. Often the sage gave instructions for a very specific course of action to correct what the sage perceived to be the soul's misalignment. Alternatively, the *refuah* (healing modality) could involve new approaches to dealing with stressful situations in the client's life. In some cases, herbal remedies were utilized.

Among the Chasidic masters of the eighteenth and nineteenth centuries, some were familiar with the healing properties of herbs. The Baal Shem Tov is said to have learned some of these skills during the time he lived in the Carpathian Mountains. His grandson, Rabbi Baruch of Medzeboz, was reputed to have used herbal remedies for his sick daughter. He believed in the hand of God operating through natural events, including choice of remedies. Jewish women of that era were also knowledgeable in the herbal area and probably incorporated that awareness into their cooking. Malka of Belz (mid-nineteenth century), who was known to be a great healer, is said to have placed her healing energy in the food that was served to the students and visitors to the Belz Chasidic court. Like the work of other women leaders in Chasidic settings, supervision of sacred meals was an important component in the sphere of the dynastic leaders. Malka's husband, Shalom Rokeach, the first Belzer Rebbe, was reputed to be able to heal schizophrenics, and he attracted people of all faiths to Belz for healing. Rebbetzin Malka probably used both herbs and *davennin* (prayer) during her supervision of the food preparation in a fashion not so different than what one would find in a Hindu ashram. In general, the rebbe's meals, which were blessed by prayers and his touch and taste, were prized by his disciples, who ate the food he had touched. In stories celebrating her life, Rebbetzin Malka is credited with using a section from the Psalms to cure a disabled man through prayer. Chanting from the Psalms is still favored by older Jewish women who pray on behalf of the sick.

The other device favored by Jewish holy men through the ages was the use of the amulet, or *kameah,* which contained a prayer written on parchment, usually of deerskin, mentioning the petitioner by name and lineage and utilizing the names of God to request a favorable outcome. Many such prayers used the forty-two-letter name of God (intoned as *Ana B Koach*) to guard the individual against negative energies. Textual amulets from rabbis or holy men were written by the saints themselves or by well-trained and observant scribes, usually following a formula passed down from ancient sources. Conceptually, all the amulet texts drew on the written versions of the sacred names of God and were designed to call the divine energy into a closer connection with the person.

There are differences of opinion about using the mezuzah (a scroll affixed to a doorway) as an amulet of protection. Although the Jewish sages explained the attachment of the prayer in a container outside the doorway of the household in legal, religious terms, there is no question but that common folk always considered it a form of protection (suggested in the Zohar) for the household and its members. The Chasidic practice of examining the mezuzah scroll for flaws and changing the scroll when someone was sick added to the aura of the mezuzah as a kind of remedy. Additionally, some individuals wore jewelry mezuzot, in the form of a necklace, as a kind of talisman.

The protection of infants—especially in times of high infant mortality—was a major focus of Jewish women. Newborn babies were traditionally wrapped with a protective binder embroidered with special Hebrew prayers. A newborn male infant required *shemira,* or guardianship from evil, prior to his circumcision ceremony. Special prayers for protection of mother and child were typical. Celebrations for the birth of girls involved calling the parents to the Torah with the infant to announce the baby girl's birth and her given Hebrew name. Another practice engaged in by women, especially in the East, was visiting the graves of relatives and saints to pray for intervention in the healing of illness. Lighting candles at the gravesite is still very popular at holy tombs in Israel. The characteristics of the buried saint would be a factor in where women would go to pray. For example, it is traditional for women to pray for children at the tomb of the matriarch Rachel outside of Bethlehem, because she struggled with fertility issues. Jewish pilgrims usually visit the tomb of Rachel on Rosh Chodesh to pray for renewed blessings and energy. Other sites have a more generic quality, including the Wailing Wall in Jerusalem and the Machpelah in Hebron, the burial place of the ancestors, dating from Abraham and Sarah. The tomb of Rabbi Meir Baal Haness (the miracle worker) in Tiberias is also a popular site to pray for health. Making pilgrimages to the tombs of saints was popular among the Jews of Islamic countries; and many sites in the Arab countries were sacred to both Jews and Muslims.

Another very important shared component in the healing iconography of Middle Eastern people was the use of the hand as an amuletic symbol and the modality for conveying the divine energy and healing power. The Jews of Arab lands were likely to craft and wear the *hamsa,* or hand of protection, possibly connected with Miriam the prophetess. The hand or *yad* is also the design on the Torah pointer, connecting to many earlier sources that refer to "the hand of God," the outstretched arm of God in the Exodus, and the hands of Moses in channeling the victorious energies of the Israelites.

The priestly blessing, traditionally given to the community in the collective prayers, is conveyed through the upstretched hands of the assembled Kohanim, the hereditary priestly families. Jewish parents also bless their children on Friday nights by placing their hands over the child's head, a practice originating in the patriarch Jacob's blessing of the children of Joseph.

All of these are examples of the Jewish custom of raising the hands in holiness to give blessings and healing. All are grounded in the belief that the upraised hands create the space where we engage the Divine Presence, Shekhinah, making it possible for the priest or the prophet to draw the Shekhinah energy to himself and convey it to others. Generations of Jewish mystics would make the connection between the ten fingers and the ten Sephirot, imbuing the human hands with the potential for drawing in the *shefa*, or flow of divine energy. Because the hands have the potential to heal as well as to do harm, some teachers considered the hand-raising gesture inappropriate if there was no intention of invoking a blessing.

Looking over this tapestry of time, we might say that Jewish practice has always involved belief in God as the ultimate healer and in the connection between body, mind, and spirit. Yet if we observed twentieth-century Jewish communities in the United States and western Europe, we might never know there was a tradition of spiritual healing in Judaism, just as we would never have heard of Shekhinah. With the resurgence of interest in spirituality and holistic health, there has also been a rebirth of Jewish healing. Some of this can be credited also to the Jewish Renewal movement, with its emphasis on nature, health, and meaningful spiritual practice. Much of this rebirth is undoubtedly a feature of our times, in which the practice of medicine has become technologically enriched but spiritually deprived.

These trends have resulted in the emergence of Jewish healing groups around the country who work in hospitals and homes to assist with the healing of specific illnesses or problems. In such contemporary Jewish groups there might be services in which the group would sing, meditate, pray, and do some sharing. These gatherings, which have become quite popular in recent years, are often an organized effort with paid chaplains. There might be special gatherings to help people dealing with AIDS, cancer, or other challenging health problems. What carries through over the ages is the desire to restore life to body, heart, and soul through channeling the abundant Shekhinah energy that surrounds us all. In the Jewish world, which has seen so much inflicted suffering, the use of words to heal has been an integral part of the healing path. The poems and prayers that have emerged from many different times in Jewish history bear witness to the amazing resilience of the human soul and the ways in which individuals grow in awareness through their ailments. In this capacity, the illness becomes the lesson, which guides a person to greater understanding of the self and a willingness to make the changes needed to bring about more vibrant health.

The reemergence of the feminine in both human and divine forms may well be the underlying cosmic ground on which all this change is based. Just as Jews lost faith in the capacity to have visions and to prophesy after the destruction of the great temples, many also lost faith in the presence of divinity in our world after the Holocaust. The contemporary emphasis on wholeness and intuition provides the opening for receiving Shekhinah energy once again. While quality health care for all and a planet in which devastating diseases can no longer obliterate large populations are still in the future, we believe they are on the way, as part of a new era that is informed by the understanding of the earth as a unified living system. We look forward to welcoming that new era.

# AYL NA REFA NA LA

by Alan Scott Bachman (Desert Wind)

Mother Shekhinah, Goddess of Light,
Heal the entire earth, end all our plight.
Your wings surround us, Divine embrace.
Cries through the many years
Healed with your grace.

AYL NA AYL NA REFA NA LA
AYL NA AYL NA
Please heal her now.

"Shekhinah," cries all creation,
"Heal our world like Miryam."
As your wings spread across all nations,
Send forth healing to everyone.

*I would like to consider the names for the Shekhinah, which are more numer-*
*ous than those of the other attributes. . . . The name of almost everything in*
*existence recalls her. . . . Each of her names reflects not the material nature,*
*heaven forbid, of the entity bearing that name but the special quality that*
*entity receives from her.*

—Rabbi Moses Cordovero, *Shiur Komah*

# *Appendix*

## Attributes and Names of Shekhinah in Zohar*

| | |
|---|---|
| angel of God | *malach elohim* |
| apple orchard | *pardes* |
| Community of Israel | Knesset Yisrael |
| crown | *atarah* |
| cup | *kos* (for *kiddush* over wine) |
| daughter of Levi | *bat ha Levi* (associated with Moses's mother, Yocheved) |
| divine bride | *ha kallah* |
| Divine Mother | Matrona, Malkhut |
| Field | *sadeh* |
| foundation stone | *even ha shetiyah* |
| Garden of Eden | *Gan Eden* |
| Glory | *kavod;* clouds of glory: *anan ha kavod* |
| heavenly voice | *bat kol* |
| hind of the dawn | *ayelet ha shachar* |
| Holy Spirit | *Ruach ha Kodesh* (associated with vision and prophecy) |
| incense | *ketoret* |
| jubilee | *yovel* (associated with the matriarch Leah) |
| light, fire | *esh* |
| mirror | *asparklaria* |
| moon | *levanah, yareach* (lesser luminary) |
| manna | *manna* (the divine food in the desert) |
| on wings of eagles | *al kanfei nesharim* (implying God's protection) |
| Oral Torah | *Torah sheh'b'al peh* |
| radiance | *ziv ha Shekhinah* |
| rainbow | *keshet* (because Shekhinah comprises many colors) |
| rose of Sharon, lily of the valley | *shoshan/shoshanim* |

# Appendix

| | |
|---|---|
| sabbatical | *bat sheva* (associated with the matriarch Rachel) |
| Shabbos Queen | *Shabbat ha malkah* |
| Tabernacle | *mishkan* (also ark, palanquin) |
| Temple | *Beit ha Mikdash* |
| throne (of God) | *ha kiseh, kiseh ha kavod* |
| thrower of light | *zarka* |
| well | *maayan* (The well is where Jacob meets Rachel, Eliezer finds Rebekah, Moses encounters Tziporah, Hagar receives the divine message, and Isaac meditates.) |
| wings, under the | |
| wings of Shekhinah | *tachat kanfei ha Shekhinah* (associated with protection and conversion) |
| womb | *rechem* |
| word | *memra, mamra, dibbur* |

*These thirty-six attributes and names for Shekhinah are but a partial list. They were drawn primarily from translations of Zohar by Dr. Daniel Matt.

# Notes on Sources

Quotations from the Zohar are taken from:

*The Zohar*, translated by Harry Sperling and Maurice Simon. New York: Soncino Press, 1984.

*The Zohar: Pritzker Edition*, translated and with commentary by Daniel C. Matt. 4 vols., covering Genesis and part of Exodus. Stanford, Calif.: Stanford University Press, 2004.

Bible quotations from Chumash (the Five Books of Moses) are from *The Torah: A Modern Commentary*, edited by W. Gunther Plaut. Jewish Publication Society. New York: Union of American Hebrew Congregations, 1981.

Prophetic quotations are from *Tanakh Yerushalayim/Jerusalem Bible*, second edition. The Tanakh includes Torah, Neviim, and Ketuvim (Five Books of Moses, Prophets, and Later Writings). Hebrew-English, Jewish Publication Society translation. Jerusalem: Koren, 1977.

Quotations from the Talmud are from *The Babylonian Talmud*, edited by I. Epstein, translated by Jacob Shachter and H. Freedman. London: Soncino Press, first published 1935.

Talmud quotations have also been taken from *Soncino Talmud*, the Babylonian Talmud in Hebrew and Aramaic with translation, Soncino edition. Davka CD-ROM from Judaica Press, Brooklyn, N.Y., 1990.

# Notes

The various sources quoted in this book use different spellings for the Divine Presence, including *Shekhina, Shekinah, Shechinah,* and *Sh'china.* In the interest of simplicity, we have standardized the spelling to that favored in Jewish academic circles, or *Shekhinah.* The style of citation from the Zohar varies based on the translated edition used as a source.

## Epigraphs for Chapter 1, page 14

"For the Shekhinah . . . " Rabbi Joseph Gikatilla, *Gates of Light: Sha'are Orah,* translated by Avi Weinstein. San Francisco: Harper Collins, 1994, p. 204.

"Every single day . . . " Zohar 1:133a (Gen. 23:1–25:18). *Zohar: Pritzker Edition,* vol. 2, p. 337.

"Now the Shekhinah . . . " Zohar 1:175b (Gen. 32:14–36:43). *The Zohar* (Soncino), vol. 2, p. 172.

"She [the Shekhinah] is sometimes . . . " Zohar 2:100b ( Exod. 21:1– 24:18). *The Zohar* (Soncino), vol. 3, p. 307.

## Epigraphs for Chapter 2, page 24

"And the Lord . . . " Exodus 13:21–2, *The Torah: A Modern Commentary.*

"The Shekhinah was accompanied . . . " Zohar 1:176b (Gen. 32:4–36:43, Num. 9:17). *The Zohar* (Soncino), vol. 2, p. 176.

"Let them build . . . " Exodus 25:8. *The Torah: A Modern Commentary.*

"And I will set . . . " Zohar 3:114a (Lev. 26:3–27:34). *The Zohar* (Soncino), vol. 5, p. 155.

## Epigraphs for Chapter 3, page 36

"She [Asherah] is worshipped . . . " Jeremiah 17:2. *Tanakh Yerushalayim/Jerusalem Bible.*

# Notes

"They bring out . . . " II Kings 23: 6. *Tanakh Yerushalayim/Jerusalem Bible.*

"May you be blessed . . . " Kuntillet Ajrud excavation, northern Sinai, 700 B.C.E. Quoted in Raphael Patai, *The Hebrew Goddess.* Detroit: Wayne State University Press, 1990, p. 53.

"The name Asherah . . . " Zohar 1:49a (Gen. 1:1–6:8). *Zohar: Pritzker Edition,* vol. 1, p. 271, n. 1264.

## Epigraphs for Chapter 4, page 50

"For the Presence . . . " I Kings 8:11-4. *Tanakh Yerushalayim/Jerusalem Bible.*

"Shekhinah in the temple . . . " Zohar 1:203a (Gen. 41:1–44:17). *The Zohar* (Soncino), vol. 2, p. 271.

"He [King Solomon] made . . . " Shir Ha Shirim Rabah 3:10, discussion of the creation of the Ark. *Midrash Rabah,* edited by H. Freedman, translated by Maurice Simon. Vol. 4 on Song of Songs. London: Soncino, first published 1977.

"The high priest . . . " Zohar 3:59a–59b (Lev. 16:1–18:30). *The Zohar* (Soncino), vol. 5, p. 41.

## Epigraphs for Chapter 5, page 58

"Shekhinah . . . at the destruction . . . " Zohar 1:203a (Gen. 41:1–44:17). *The Zohar* (Soncino), vol. 2, p. 271.

"Shekhinah never leaves . . . " Zohar 3:66a (Lev. 16:1–18:30). *The Zohar* (Soncino), vol. 5, p. 59.

"A judge who delivers . . . " Sanhedrin 7a. *The Babylonian Talmud.*

"Whenever Torah is studied . . . " Zohar 1:115b (Gen. 18:1–22:24). *The Zohar* (Soncino), vol. 1, p. 361.

## Epigraphs for Chapter 6, page 68

"According to his will . . . " Rabbi El'azar ben Yehudah of Worms (1160–1230), *Sefer Rokeach.* Quoted in Joseph Dan, *The Heart and the Fountain: An Anthology of Jewish Mystical Experiences.* New York: Oxford University Press, 2002, chapter 8, p. 112, "Rokeah: Devotion in Prayer."

# Notes

"Prayer is God's partner . . . " Rabbi El'azar ben Yehudah of Worms, *Sefer Ha Hochmah.* Quoted in Joseph Dan, *Jewish Mysticism,* vol. 2. Northvale, N.J.: Aronson, 1998, p. 256.

"It is a form . . . " Saadia Gaon, *The Book of Beliefs and Opinions,* translated by Samuel Rosenblatt. New Haven: Yale Judaica Series, 1976, p. 121.

## Tree of Life diagram, Chapter 7, page 78

The attributes listed on the diagram are my contemporary variations on the classical terms for the Sephirot, with appreciation to R. Steven Fisdel for his insightful mapping of the tree in modern psychological terms (*The Practice of Kabbalah*).

Postmedieval Kabbalists, including Rabbi Moses Cordovero (1522–70) and Rabbi Joseph Tzayach (1505–73), connected the various names of God to the Sephirot; Cordovero also had a system of color designations that can be found in Rabbi Fisdel's book. New Age books on the Tree of Life tend to provide colors for each Sephira that are aligned with Western Theosophical teachings. The Zohar does mention white for Chesed and red for Gevurah, and sometimes refers to Shekhinah as the rainbow comprising many colors. The Zohar sometimes connects the color blue with Shekhinah, related to the color of sea and sky.

In classical Kabbalah, the patriarchs are assigned to specific Sephirot, with Abraham in Chesed, Isaac in Gevurah, and Jacob in Tiferet. The Zohar places Rachel and King David in Malkhut and refers to Leah in Binah. I usually add Rebekah in Gevurah and Sarah in Tiferet or Hod. Contemporary feminist scholars have considered attributions for the seven women prophets mentioned in the Talmud (Sarah, Devorah, Avigail, Miriam, Chanah, Huldah, and Queen Esther). While there is no "official" version, the scheme developed by author Tamar Frankiel (*The Gift of Kabbalah*) is closest to my thinking. In this formulation, she places Miriam in Chesed, Huldah in Gevurah, Sarah in Tiferet, Devorah in Netzach, Chanah in Hod, Avigail in Yesod, and Queen Esther in Malkhut. Others add Tamar in Yesod because of her sexual role, as described in Genesis. These designations are used in the ritual known as Ushpizin for welcoming ancestral guests into the sukka arbor for the fall Feast of Booths.

## Epigraphs for Chapter 8, page 92

"On this Sabbath night . . . " Elliot Ginsburg, *The Sabbath in the Classical Kabbalah.* Albany, N.Y.: State University of New York Press, 1989, p. 131. Based on Zohar 2:204a.

"The Supernal Holy One . . . " Ginsburg, *The Sabbath in the Classical Kabbalah,* p. 131. Based on Zohar 1:48a.

# Notes

"This tabernacle of peace . . . " Zohar 1:48a (Gen. 1:1–6:8). *The Zohar* (Soncino), vol. 1, p. 153.

"Ribono Shel Olam . . . " Sarah Bas Tovim, "Shlosha Shearim" (Three Gates), candle-lighting prayer, in Rivka Zakutinsky, *Techinas: A Voice from the Heart*, vol. 2. (Brooklyn, N.Y.: Aura, 1999, p. 217.

"For the Sabbath . . . " *Rayya Meheimna* 3:272b quoted in Elliot K. Ginsburg, *The Sabbath in the Classical Kabbalah*. New York: State Univ. of New York Press, 1989, p. 117.

## Epigraphs for Chapter 9, page 104

"It is the Tsaddik . . . " Moshe Idel, *Hasidism: Between Ecstasy and Magic*. Albany, N.Y.: State University of New York Press, 1995, p. 200.

"Think yourself as nothing . . . " Rabbi Dov Baer, Maggid of Mezeritch. Quoted in Leonora Leet, *Renewing the Covenant: A Kabbalistic Guide to Jewish Spirituality*. Rochester, Vt.: Inner Traditions, 1999. Based on Aryeh Kaplan, *The Light Beyond: Adventures in Hassidic Thought*. Brooklyn, N.Y.: Maznaim, 1981, p. 158.

"Only the prayer . . . " Baal Shem Tov. Quoted in Martin Buber, *The Legend of the Baal Shem*, translated by Maurice Friedman. New York: Schocken Books, 1969, pp. 27, 32.

"Understand that just as . . . " Rabbi Dov Baer, Maggid of Mezeritch, *Haim V Hesed* 10. Quoted in *God in All Moments: Mystical and Practical Spiritual Wisdom from Hasidic Masters*, edited and translated by Or Rose with Ebn. D. Leader. Woodstock, Vt.: Jewish Lights Publishing, 2004, p. 43.

## Epigraphs for Chapter 10, page 116

"Take me in . . . " Chaim Nachman Bialik (1834–1904, Israel's national poet), "Place Me Under Your Wing," in *Songs from Bialik: Selected Poems of Chaim Nachman Bialik*, translated by Atar Hadari. Syracuse, N.Y.: Syracuse University Press, 2000.

"Modest are the gifts . . . " Rachel Blaustein, "To My Country," in *The Defiant Muse: Hebrew Feminist Poems*, edited by Galit Haskam Rokan and Tamar S. Hess, translated by Robert Friend. New York: The Feminist Press of CUNY, 1999, p. 85.

# Notes

"And if you ask . . . " Saul Tchernikovsky (1875–1943, Haskalah poet). Quoted in Roger Gottlieb, *This Sacred Earth: Religion, Nature, and the Environment.* New York: Routledge, 1996, p. 95.

"And when you . . . " A. D. Gordon (1856–1922, Israeli writer), *Mivhar Ketavim* 57–59. Quoted in Daniel Schwartz, "Jews, Jewish Texts, and Nature," COEJL (Coalition on the Environment and Jewish life) Web site, http://coejl.org/learn/je_swartz.php.

## Epigraphs for Chapter 11, page 128

"We are the tree . . . " Hanna Tiferet Siegel (Hornby Island, BC, Canada), "In the Garden of Shekhinah" (song).

"Barchu, Dear One . . . " Lev Friedman (Boston, Mass.), modern *barchu* (call to prayer), based on a Sufi melody.

"Open to me . . . " Aryeh Hirschfeld (Portland, Ore.), "Open to Me" (song).

"*Bruchot habaot tachat* . . . " Debbie Friedman, "Bruchot Habaot" (welcoming song), in *Blessings.* New York: SoundsWrite Productions, 1990.

## Epigraphs for Chapter 12, page 140

"Before a man dies . . . " Zohar 3:88b (Lev. 21:2–24:23). *The Zohar* (Soncino), vol. 5.

"Nor does the soul . . . " Zohar 3:53a (Lev. 14:1–15:33). *The Zohar* (Soncino), vol. 5, p. 26.

"When the spirit . . . " Zohar 3:126b (Num. 4: 21–7:89). *The Zohar* (Soncino), vol. 5, p. 187.

"In the future world . . . " Berachot 17a. *The Babylonian Talmud.*

## Epigraphs for Chapter 13, page 148

"Rabbi Akiva expounded . . . " Sotah 17a. *The Babylonian Talmud.*

"When sexual relations . . . " Sotah 17a. Babylonian Talmud. Quoted in David Biale, *Eros and the Jews.* New York: Basic Books, 1992, p. 58.

# Notes

"When union is . . . " *Igeret Ha Kodesh,* attributed to Nachmanides. *The Holy Letter: A Study in Medieval Jewish Sexual Morality,* edited and translated by Seymour J. Cohen. New York: Ktav, 1976, p. 5.

"Where there is . . . " Zohar 3:59a–b (Lev. 16:1–18:30). *The Zohar* (Soncino), vol. 5.

## Epigraphs for Chapter 14, page 156

"If one dreams . . . " Berachot 57a. *The Babylonian Talmud.*

"A person should remember . . . " Zohar 1:200a (Gen. 41:1–44:17). *The Zohar* (Pritzer Edition), vol. 3, p. 225.

"A man is shown . . . " Berachot 55b. *The Babylonian Talmud.*

"When a man is . . . " Zohar 3:67a (Lev. 16:1–18:30). *The Zohar* (Soncino), vol. 5, p. 61.

## Epigraphs for Chapter 15, page 166

"Whoever pronounces . . . " Sanhedrin 42a. *The Babylonian Talmud.*

"You have given us . . . " Leah Horowitz, "Tkhine for the New Moon," in Chava Weissler, *Voices of the Matriarchs.* Boston: Beacon, 1998, pp. 117–8.

"May it be . . . " Rabbi Eliezer Toledano, *Orot Sephardic Shabbat Siddur.* Lakewood, N.J.: Orot, 2002, p. 439. Prayer for announcing the new moon.

"God's crescent kiss . . . " Susan Berrin, editor, *Celebrating the New Moon: A Rosh Chodesh Anthology.* Northvale, N.J.: Aronson, 1996, dedication.

## Epigraphs for Chapter 16, page 174

"The Shekhinah hovers . . . " Shabbat 12b. *The Babylonian Talmud.*

"When we perform . . . " Estelle Frankel, *Sacred Therapy: Jewish Spiritual Teachings on Emotional Healing and Inner Wholeness.* Boston: Shambhala, 2003, p. 245.

"The divine Presence . . . " Shabbat 30b. *The Babylonian Talmud,* footnote commentary to II Kings 3:15.

# Notes

"Nature does not operate . . . " Rabbi Baruch of Medzeboz (grandson of the Baal Shem Tov). Quoted in Rivka Zakutinsky, *Techinas: A Voice from the Heart—A Collection of Women's Prayers.* vol. 3. Brooklyn, N.Y.: Aura, 1999, p. 450.

## Epigraph for Appendix, page 184

"I would like . . . " Rabbi Moses Cordovero, *Shiur Komah*, sec. 27, fol. 42b. Quoted in Moshe Hallamish, *An Introduction to the Kabbalah,* translated by Ruth Bar-Ilan and Orah Wiskind-Elper. Albany, N.Y.: State University of New York Press, 1999.

# Bibliography

Abelson, Joshua. *The Immanence of God in Rabbinical Literature.* New York: Hermon, 1912 (1969 printing).

Adelman, Penina Villenchik. *Miriam's Well: Rituals for Jewish Women Around the Year.* Fresh Meadows, N.Y.: Biblio, 1986.

Antonelli, Judith S. *In the Image of God: A Feminist Commentary on Torah.* Northvale, N.J.: Aronson, 1995.

Aron, Milton. *Ideas and Ideals of the Hassidim.* New York: Citadel, 1969.

Bakan, David. *And They Took Themselves Wives: The Emergence of Patriarchy in Western Civilization.* San Francisco: Harper and Row, 1979.

Ben-Amos, Dan, and Jerome Mintz, trans. and ed. *In Praise of the Baal Shem Tov: The Earliest Collection of Legends About the Founder of Hasidism.* New York: Schocken Books, 1984.

Berrin, Susan, ed. *Celebrating the New Moon: A Rosh Chodesh Anthology.* Northvale, N.J.: Aronson, 1996.

Besserman, Perle. *New Kabbalah for Women.* New York: Palgrave Macmillan, 2005.

Biale, David. *Eros and the Jews: From Biblical Israel to Contemporary America.* New York: Basic Books, 1992.

Boyarin, Daniel. *Carnal Israel: Reading Sex in Talmudic Culture.* Berkeley: University of California Press, 1993.

Buber, Martin. *The Legend of the Baal-Shem.* Translated from the German by Maurice Friedman. Princeton, N.J.: Princeton University Press, 1995.

Bulka, Reuven P. *Judaism on Pleasure.* Northvale, N.J.: Aronson, 1995.

Buxbaum, Yitzhak. *The Light and Fire of the Baal Shem Tov.* New York: Continuum, 2005.

Cohen, Seymour J., trans. *The Holy Letter: A Study in Jewish Sexual Morality.* Northvale, N.J.: Aronson, c. 1993.

Cordovero, Moshe. *The Palm Tree of Devorah.* Translated and annotated by Moshe Miller. Southfield, Mich.: Targum, 1994.

Covitz, Joel. *Visions of the Night: A Study of Jewish Dream Interpretation.* Boston: Shambhala, 1990.

Dan, Joseph, ed. *The Heart and the Fountain: An Anthology of Jewish Mystical Experiences.* New York: Oxford University Press, 2002.

# Bibliography

Dan, Joseph. *Jewish Mysticism*. Vol. 1, *Late Antiquity*, and vol. 2, *The Middle Ages*. Northvale N.J.: Aronson, 1998.

Deutsch, Nathaniel. *The Maiden of Ludmir: A Jewish Holy Woman and Her World*. Berkeley: University of California Press, 2003.

Diamant, Anita. *The Red Tent*. New York: St. Martin's Press, 1997.

Dosick, Wayne and Ellen Kaufman Dosick. *20 Minute Kabbalah*. Cardiff by the Sea, Calif.: Waterside Publishing, 2007.

Dossey, Larry. *Healing Words: The Power of Prayer and the Practice of Medicine*. San Francisco: HarperCollins, 1993.

Falk, Marcia. *The Book of Blessings*. San Francisco: HarperSanFrancisco, 1996.

Finkel, Avraham Yaakov. *The Great Chasidic Masters*. Northvale, N.J.: Aronson, 1996.

Firestone, R. Tirzah. *The Receiving: Reclaiming Jewish Women's Wisdom*. San Francisco: HarperOne, 2003.

Fisdel, Steven A. *The Practice of Kabbalah: Meditation in Judaism*. Northvale, N.J.: Aronson, 1996.

Frankel, Estelle. *Sacred Therapy: Jewish Spiritual Teachings on Emotional Healing and Inner Wholeness*. Shambhala: Boston, 2003.

Frankiel, Tamar. *The Gift of Kabbalah: Discovering the Secrets of Heaven, Renewing Your Life on Earth*. Woodstock, Vt.: Jewish Lights, 2001.

Gikatilla, Joseph Ben Abraham. *Gates of Light*. Translated by Avi Weinstein. San Francisco: HarperCollins, 1994.

Ginsburg, Elliott Kiba. *The Sabbath in the Classical Kabbalah*. Albany: State University of New York Press, 1989.

Ginzberg, Louis. *Legends of the Jews*. New York: Simon and Schuster, 1956.

Goldstein, Elyse, ed. *The Women's Torah Commentary: New Insights from Women Rabbis on the 54 Weekly Torah Portions*. Woodstock, Vt.: Jewish Lights, 2000.

Gottlieb, Freema. *The Lamp of God: A Jewish Book of Light*. Northvale, N.J.: Aronson, 1996.

Gottlieb, Lynn. *She Who Dwells Within: A Feminist Vision of a Renewed Judaism*. San Francisco: HarperOne, 1995.

Green, Arthur. *Ehyeh: A Kabbalah for Tomorrow*. Woodstock, Vt.: Jewish Lights, 2003.

Green, Arthur, and Barry Noltz, eds. and trans. *Your Word Is Fire: The Hasidic Masters on Contemplative Prayer*. New York: Schocken Books, 1987.

Greenberg, Blu. *On Women and Judaism: A View from Tradition*. Philadelphia: Jewish Publication Society, 1994.

# Bibliography

Hallamish, Moshe. *An Introduction to the Kabbalah*. Translated by Ruth Bar-Ilan and Ora Wiskind-Elper. Albany: State University of New York Press, 1999.

Hammer, Jill. *Sisters at Sinai: New Tales of Biblical Women*. Philadelphia: Jewish Publication Society, 2001.

Heschel, Abraham Joshua. *The Sabbath: Its Meaning for Modern Man*. New York: Farrar, Straus and Giroux, 1996.

Heschel, Susannah. *On Being a Jewish Feminist*. New York: Schocken Books, 1983.

Idel, Moshe. *Hasidism: Between Ecstasy and Magic*. Albany: State University of New York Press, 1995.

———. *Kabbalah: New Perspectives*. New Haven: Yale University Press, 1988.

Jacobs, Louis. *Jewish Mystical Testimonies*. New York: Schocken Books, 1976.

*Jerusalem Bible: Tanakh Yerushalayim* (bilingual), 2nd ed. Translated by Harold Fisch. Jerusalem: Koren, 1977.

Johnson, Elizabeth A. *She Who Is: The Mystery of God in a Feminist Theological Discourse*. New York: Crossroad, 1992.

Kaplan, Aryeh. *Jewish Meditation: A Practical Guide*. New York: Schocken Books, 1985.

———, ed. and trans. *Meditation and Kabbalah*. York Beach, Maine: Samuel Weiser, 1993.

Klapheck, Elisa. *Fraülein Rabbiner Jonas: The Story of the First Woman Rabbi*. Translated by Toby Axelrod. San Francisco: Jossey-Bass/John Wiley & Sons, 2004.

Klein, Eliahu. *Kabbalah of Creation: Isaac Luria's Earlier Mysticism*. Northvale, N.J.: Aronson, 2000.

———. *Meetings with Remarkable Souls: Legends of the Baal Shem Tov*. Northvale, N.J.: Aronson, 1995.

Kook, Abraham Isaac. *Celebration of the Soul*. Translated by Pesach Jaffe. Jerusalem: Genesis Jerusalem Press, 1992.

Leet, Leonora. *Renewing the Covenant: A Kabbalistic Guide to Jewish Spirituality*. Rochester, N.Y.: Inner Traditions, 1999.

Lipschitz, Chaim U. *Kiddush L'vono: The Monthly Blessing of the Moon*. Brooklyn, N.Y.: Maznaim, 1987.

Long, Asphodel P. *In a Chariot Drawn by Lions: The Search for the Female in Deity*. Freedom, Calif.: Crossing Press, 1993.

Luzzato, Moses. *General Principles of the Kabbalah*. Translated by the Research Centre of Kabbalah. New York: Press of the Research Centre of Kabbalah, 1970.

Matt, Daniel C. *The Essential Kabbalah: The Heart of Jewish Mysticism*. San Francisco: Harper, 1996.

# Bibliography

————. *The Zohar: Pritzker Edition.* 4 vols. Palo Alto, Calif.: Stanford University Press, 2004–2007.

Mintz, Jerome R. *Legends of the Hasidim: An Introduction to Hasidic Culture and Oral Tradition in the New World.* Chicago: Chicago University Press, 1968.

Moss, Robert. *Dreamgates: An Explorer's Guide to the Worlds of Soul, Imagination and Life Beyond Death.* New York: Three Rivers, 1998.

Moss, Robert. *The Three "Only" Things: Tapping the Power of Dreams, Coincidence and Imagination.* Novato, Calif.: New World Library, 2007.

Nicholson, Shirley, ed. *The Goddess Reawakening: The Feminine Principle Today.* Wheaton, Ill.: Theosophical Publishing House, 1989.

Patai, Jozsef, trans. *Souls and Secrets: Hasidic Stories.* Northvale, N.J.: Aronson, 1995.

Patai, Raphael. *The Hebrew Goddess.* Detroit: Wayne State University Press, 1990.

Pirani, Alix, ed. *The Absent Mother.* London: Mandala, 1991.

Plaskow, Judith, and Carol P. Christ. *Weaving the Visions: New Patterns in Feminist Spirituality.* San Francisco: Harper and Row, 1989.

Porten, Bezalel. *Archives from Elephantine: The Life of an Ancient Jewish Military Colony.* Berkeley: University of California Press, 1968.

Rabinowics, Tzvi. *The Encyclopedia of Hasidism.* Northvale, N.J.: Aronson, 1996.

Ribner, Melinda. *Kabbalah Month by Month: A Year of Spiritual Practice and Personal Transformation.* San Francisco: Jossey-Bass, 2002.

Rose, Or, with Ebn. D. Leader, eds. and trans. *God in All Moments: Mystical and Practical Spiritual Wisdom from Hasidic Masters.* Woodstock, Vt.: Jewish Lights, 2004.

Ruether, Rosemary Radford. *Gaia and God: An Ecofeminist Theology of Earth Healing.* San Francisco: Harper, 1994.

Saadia Gaon. *The Book of Belief and Opinions.* Translated by Samuel Rosenblatt. Vol. 1, Yale Judaica Series. New Haven and London: Yale University Press, 1976.

Sanford, John A. *Dreams: God's Forgotten Language.* Philadelphia: Lippincott, 1968.

Schachter-Shalomi, Zalman. *Spiritual Intimacy: A Study of Counseling in Hasidism.* Northvale, N.J.: Aronson, 1991.

————. *Wrapped in a Holy Flame: Teachings and Tales of the Hasidic Masters.* Edited by Nataniel M. Miles-Yepez. San Francisco: Jossey-Bass, 2003.

Schafer, Peter. *The Hidden and Manifest God: Some Major Themes in Early Jewish Mysticism.* Translated by Aubrey Pomerance. Albany: State University of New York Press, 1992.

Scholem, Gershom. *On the Kabbalah and Its Symbolism.* New York: Schocken Books, 1965.

# Bibliography

———. *On the Mystical Shape of the Godhead: Basic Concepts in the Kabbalah.* Translated from the German by Joachim Neugroschel. New York: Schocken Books, 1991.

———. *Origins of the Kabbalah.* Edited by R. J. Werblowsky, translated by Allan Arkush. Philadelphia: Jewish Publication Society, 1987.

Shapiro, Rami. *The Divine Feminine in Biblical Wisdom Literature.* Woodstock, Vt.: Skylight Paths, 2005.

Sherbok, Dan Cohn, ed. *Jewish Mysticism: An Anthology.* Rockport, Mass.: Oneworld, 1995.

Shulman, Y. David *The Sefirot: Ten Emanations of Divine Power.* Northvale, N.J.: Aronson, 1996.

Teubal, Savina J. *Hagar the Egyptian: The Lost Tradition of the Matriarchs.* San Francisco: Harper, 1990.

———. *Sarah the Priestess: The First Matriarch of Genesis.* Athens, Ohio: Swallow, 1984.

Tishby, Isaiah, ed., with Fischel Lachower. *The Wisdom of the Zohar: An Anthology of Texts.* 3 vols. Translated by David Goldstein. Washington, D.C.: Littman Library of Jewish Civilization, 1994.

*The Torah: A Modern Commentary.* Edited by W. Gunther Plaut. New York: Jewish Publication Society, 1981.

Trachtenberg, Joshua. *Jewish Magic and Superstition: A Study in Folk Religion.* New York: Atheneum, 1974.

Urbach, Efraim Elimelech. *The Sages: World and Wisdom of the Rabbis of the Talmud.* Boston: Harvard University Press, 1987.

Weissler, Chava. *Voices of the Matriarchs: Listening to the Prayers of Early Modern Jewish Women.* Boston: Beacon, 1998.

Westheimer, Ruth Karola, and Jonathan Mark. *Heavenly Sex: Sexuality in the Jewish Tradition.* New York: New York University Press, 1995.

Wiener, Shohama. *The Fifty-Eighth Century: A Jewish Renewal Sourcebook.* Northvale, N.J.: Aronson, 1996.

Wiesel, Elie. *Souls on Fire: Portraits and Legends of Hasidic Masters.* Translated from the French by Marion Wiesel. New York: Vintage Books, 1972.

Winkler, Gershon. *Magic of the Ordinary: Recovering the Shamanic in Judaism.* Berkeley, Calif.: North Atlantic Books, 2003.

Winston, Jerry. *The Mystical Sabbath.* San Francisco: Barah Books, 1991.

Wolfson, Elliot Reuben. *Along the Path: Studies in Kabbalistic Myth, Symbolism and Hermeneutics.* Albany: State University of New York Press, 1995.

# Bibliography

———. *Through a Speculum That Shines: Vision and Imagination in Medieval Jewish Mysticism*. Princeton, N.J.: Princeton University Press, 1994.

Zakutinsky, Rivka. *Techinas: A Voice from the Heart*. Brooklyn, N.Y.: Aura, 1999.

*Zohar with Sulam Commentary by Rav Yehudah Ashlag*. Aramaic and English, 24 vols. Edited and compiled by Michael Berg. Kabbalah Center International, 2003.

*The Zohar.* Harry Sperling and Maurice Simon, eds. and trans. New York: Soncino, 1984.

# Index

# Index

# Index

# Index

# Index

# Index

# Index

# Index

Related Quest Titles
*Judaism*, by Jay G. Williams
*Kabbalah: Your Path to Inner Freedom*, by Ann Williams-Heller

**Rabbi Léah Novick** has been widely honored for her pathfinding work in bringing the Divine Feminine into contemporary Jewish liturgy and rituals. One of the eldest among the almost one-thousand women rabbis, she was ordained in 1987 by Rabbi Zalman Schachter-Shalomi, the master teacher of the Jewish Renewal Movement. Since then her teaching and research has focused primarily on the Shekhinah. This book assembles the important knowledge Rabbi Léah has acquired on the subject and combines it with guided visualizations drawn from her many successful workshops and ceremonies. She also writes about Jewish women saints, and that work has evolved into theatrical performance with her advanced students.

Rabbi Léah lives on California's Central Coast, where she draws inspiration from the beauty of the natural environment. Her deeply ecumenical lifestyle has enabled her to experience the Divine Feminine in many spiritual traditions. It is this quality she hopes to share with her readers.

"Rabbi Léah is a prophetic vessel through whom Shekhinah's voice is rebirthed. If we listen to the sweet words and wise teachings and embrace the Sheltering Presence, we can become holy partners in braiding the Divine Masculine and the Divine Feminine into Oneness, so that, once again, God will be in Fullness and Earth will be Eden."

—Rabbi Wayne Dosick, Ph.D., author of *Living Judaism*,
*Soul Judaism*, and *20 Minute Kabbalah*